Against Illiberalism

Against Illiberalism

A critique of illiberal trends in liberal institutions, with a focus on Unitarian Universalism

David Cycleback

Against Illiberalism
by David Cycleback (ברוך בן אברהם ושרה)
Center for Artifact Studies
© 2022, David Cycleback, all rights reserved
ISBN: 9798841275626

Acknowledgments to Sandra Rudd and Rev. Richard Trudeau for reviewing the text, Sophia Carey (Yale University) and Catarina Amorim (Oxford University) for their input, Dick Burkhart for reviewing an earlier paper, and to Jim Aikin for his editing services.

"I want to defend society and its inhabitants from all ideologies, science included. All ideologies must be seen in perspective. One must not take them too seriously. One must read them like fairy-tales which have lots of interesting things to say but which also contain wicked lies, or like ethical prescriptions which may be useful rules of thumb but which are deadly when followed to the letter." — philosopher of science Paul Feyerabend

"I just fundamentally believe that we should be fighting for a world in which there are no caste systems, in which people are judged based on their individual merit and character, in which we move from the historical construct of race, rather than reifying it. I just don't think you look at history and believe making people fixated on their immutable characteristics and saying those immutable characteristics have immutable power leads to anywhere good."— Bari Weiss, author of *How to Fight Antisemitism*

Against Illiberalism

Contents

About the author

1 Introduction

2 What Is Unitarian Universalism?

3 Lack of Racial Diversity in UU

4 There is No One Answer to What to Do

5 Recent Radical Attempts at Change in UU and the Introduction of Critical Race Theory

6 Positive Aspects of CRT

7 Common Criticisms of Critical Race Theory

8 Is CRT Itself Illiberal, or Is CRT Just Sometimes Applied Illiberally?

9 These All Are Topics for Discussion and Debate

10 Extreme Social Justice Activism as a Religion

11 Language as an Ideological Tool

12 Intolerance and Illiberalism: How to Make Universities Mediocre

13 Intolerance and Illiberalism in Unitarian Universalism

14 A Jewish Perspective

15 Why the UUA Is Probably Doomed to Fail in Its Goals

16 Conclusion

Appendix
   Appendix 1.1: "Standing on the Side of Power" by Munro Sickafoose
   Appendix 1.2: "I vs. We" by Jim Aikin

Against Illiberalism

About the author

David Cycleback (ברוך בן אברהם ושרה) Ph.D. is Director of Center for Artifact Studies and a member of the British Royal Institute of Philosophy. He is the author of ten university textbooks in cognitive science and philosophy, including *Cognitive Science of Religion and Belief Systems, Nature and Limits of Human Knowledge,* and *Philosophy of Artificial Intelligence.*

1 Introduction

This text examines recent illiberal trends in traditionally liberal American institutions. It critiques illiberal "anti-racism" approaches based on critical race theory (CRT) and the ideas of academics such as Ibram X. Kendi and Robin DiAngelo. It also focuses on Unitarian Universalism, a historically liberal American church whose national leadership has adopted a dogmatic, authoritarian version of critical race theory as a "theological mandate," causing strife and division.

Inequalities, unfairness, and prejudices are problems in all societies throughout human history. Stereotyping, unconscious biases, and tribalism are innate in human psychology and society. There is no single or objectively correct answer to addressing disparities. There is also no single or objectively correct way to organize societies, communities, and organizations.

While critical race theory (CRT) offers insights on racism and society, I believe in liberalism*, freedom of speech, and the free exchange of ideas, things that extreme CRT adherents oppose. Freedom of speech and expression and the respectful exchange of ideas inherently support diversity, multiculturalism, and minorities. Illiberalism, dogmatism, and authoritarianism are oppressive of all groups, minority and majority, and should be rejected wherever they appear.

As there are no simple or objective answers, this book encourages discussion. The most intolerable aspect of recent illiberal trends, and a key reason for my writing this book, is the stifling of debate and of the exchange of ideas.

* **Definition of liberalism in this text**: The definition of liberalism in this text and generally throughout the world differs from the common American definition. Americans commonly associate the terms "liberalism" and "liberal" with the political left and the Democratic Party.

Often referred to as *classical liberalism*, liberalism in this text and generally in the world refers to a political and moral philosophy that supports, amongst other things, individual and human rights, equality, democracy, freedom of belief, economic and political freedom, and freedom of speech and the press. This form of liberalism includes people from the political left, center, and right.

Liberal religion or **religious liberalism** is liberalism in the context of religion and church. It contrasts with fundamentalist, dogmatic, and orthodox religions such as Catholicism and Calvinism.

Illiberalism means opposition to or lack of liberalism. Illiberalism includes opposition to or lack of freedom of thought and behavior, and lack of civil liberties. It is associated with fundamentalism, dogmatism, and intolerance. Illiberalism is found in both the political right and the political left.

2 What Is Unitarian Universalism?

Unitarian Universalism (UU) is a liberal church formed in 1961 by combining the centuries-old Unitarian and Universalist denominations. Unitarianism in particular has a long heretical tradition dating back to Michael Servetus, who was burned at the stake by John Calvin for renouncing the ideas of the Trinity and original sin. UU does not have a creed but has a basic set of ethical principles including freedom of conscience and the use of democratic processes, beliefs in the inherent dignity and worth of every person and the interdependent web of the universe, and the free and responsible search for truth. (Furrer 2019) (UU Humanist Association 2018)

UU minister Rev. Rick Davis wrote, "In founding our two traditions our Universalist and Unitarian forebears sought to create a religious refuge from the oppressive attitudes and practices engendered by ideological, dogmatic thinking."

University of Chicago evolutionary biology professor and religion critic Jerry Coyne wrote, "Of all existing religions that claim to be religions, Unitarian Universalism (UU) seems to be the least dogmatic and therefore the least harmful—and perhaps the most liberal and tolerant."

While Unitarians and Universalists were historically Christian, modern UU is pluralistic. Its theological sources come from different religious and secular traditions. Its membership includes Christians, Jews, Muslims, agnostics, atheists, Buddhists, Hindus, and pagans. A UU slogan is, "We don't have to think alike to love alike."

An example of the pluralism and UU's principle of "the free and responsible search for truth" is the *Build Your Own Theology* classes held by many congregations. Designed by Rev. Dr. Richard S. Gilbert, the program is described as: "Based on the assumption that everyone is their own theologian, this classic UU adult education program invites participants to develop their own personal credos, the fundamental religious beliefs, values, and convictions that inform and direct of their lives." (inSpirit 2015)

Unlike top-down churches such as Catholicism, UU congregations are independent, self-determining, and laity-led, democratically picking their ministers. Traditionally, the national organization, the Unitarian Universalist Association (UUA), has worked as a service organization to support congregations. (WSUU 2016)

Social justice work has long been a part of UU. UU has been active in the abolitionist and civil rights movement, women's and LGBT+ rights, and anti-nuclear, anti-war, and environmental causes. It was the first major church to perform homosexual unions, and the first traditionally white-dominant American church to have a black person lead the national organization. More of the ministers are women than men. (UUA 2016) (UUA 2017) (UU World 2011)

UU is small, eccentric, and shrinking. Its pluralism, including the inclusion of atheists and agnostics, lack of central theology, and increasingly left politics make it the perfect church for a small minority of people, but too fringe and politically narrow for most Americans. (UUA 2020) (Loehr 2005) (Halsted 2019) (UUA 1997) (Loehr 2005) (Halsted 2018) (UUA 2018)

References

Furrer, S. (2019), "From the Minister: We Are Heretics," https://esuc.org/from-the-minister-we-are-heretics/

Gregg, C. (2013), "Building Your Own Theology," https://www.frederickuu.org/sermons/BuildingTheology.pdf

Halsted, J. (2019), "My Church is Dying and I'm OK with that," https://praywithyourfeet.org/2019/12/17/my-church-is-dying-and-im-ok-with-that/

inSpirit (2015), "Building Your Own Theology, Volume 1," https://www.uuabookstore.org/Building-Your-Own-Theology-Volume-1-P16645.aspx

Loehr, D. (2005), "Why Unitarian Universalism is Dying," https://files.meadville.edu/files/resources/why-unitarian-universalism-is-dying.pdf

Unitarian Universalist Association (2017), "Social Justice," https://www.uua.org/leaderlab/learning-center/governance/polity/47013.shtml

UU Humanist Association (2018), "The Freethinker Friendly Program," https://huumanists.org/programs/freethinker-friendly

UU World (2011), "Key moments in UUA History," https://www.uuworld.org/articles/key-uua-history

UUA (2020), "UUA Membership Statistics, 1961-2020," https://www.uua.org/data/demographics/uua-statistics

WSUU (2016), "Governance & Policies," https://wsuu.org/governance-policies/

3 Lack of Racial Diversity in UU

Unitarian Universalism (UU) is far whiter than the United States population and Christian and conservative churches, including the Catholics, Jehovah's Witnesses, the Anglican Church, and Mormons. While UU has advanced from its heterosexual, patriarchal roots, the lack of racial diversity has been a source of angst to many UUs, who see themselves as in the social justice vanguard. (UUA 2010) (Braestrup 2017) (Pew Research Center 2015)

As with most churches, Unitarian Universalism has had a particular demographic and culture. UU is often associated with its white, Puritan, New England roots. Famous Unitarians include Ralph Waldo Emerson, Henry David Thoreau, Susan B. Anthony, Thomas Jefferson, Frank Lloyd Wright, Kurt Vonnegut, and Julian Jaynes. The Collegeville Pennsylvania fellowship is named after Thomas Paine.

Martin Luther King Jr. said that Sunday at 11 a.m. is the most segregated time in America, with people traditionally tending to congregate with their own demographic. Some racial minorities have said they are drawn to UU's beliefs but have difficulty fitting in with the dominant culture. One congregant wrote, "I don't think segregation is intentional. It's a matter of music, demographics, age, culture, worship style, etc." (Blake 2010) (Grossman 2015) (8th Principle)

Anyone who attends a UU congregation knows they are likely to have a controlled, insular, polite, Northern European-American culture. As a native of Wisconsin and with many Minnesotan relatives, I've commented that the culture of the UU congregation I attend is "very Scandinavian."

I am neurodivergent (autistic and bipolar) and Jewish, and from personal experience I understand how people who are different can feel frustrated and misunderstood in a UU congregation's culture and controlled structure. Working in a multi-racial workplace, belonging to a multi-ethnic extended family, and having attended an interfaith seminary with students and professors of various religious, ethnic, and national backgrounds, I know how fulfilling diverse spaces can be. I agree with the UUA that UUs should work on being educated about different cultures and peoples and learn to be welcoming to all who are attracted to UU's beliefs.

References

8th Principle, "Where Did This Come From Originally?", https://www.8thprincipleuu.org/background

Blake, J. (2010), "Why Sunday morning remains America's most segregated hour," https://religion.blogs.cnn.com/2010/10/06/why-sunday-morning-remains-americas-most-segregated-hour/

Braestrup, K. (2017), "Where Are We Headed?", https://trulyopenmindsandhearts.blog/2017/11/21/where-are-we-headed/

Grossman, C. (2015), "Sunday Is Still the Most Segregated Day of the Week," https://www.americamagazine.org/content/all-things/sunday-still-most-segregated-day-week

Halsted, J. (2019), "My Church is Dying and I'm OK with that," https://praywithyourfeet.org/2019/12/17/my-church-is-dying-and-im-ok-with-that/

Loehr, D. (2005), "Why Unitarian Universalism is Dying," https://files.meadville.edu/files/resources/why-unitarian-universalism-is-dying.pdf

McCardle, E. (2017), "Two-thirds of UU congregations participate in White Supremacy Teach-In," https://www.uuworld.org/articles/two-thirds-participate-teach

Pew Research Center (2015), "The most and least racially diverse U.S. religious groups," https://www.pewresearch.org/fact-tank/2015/07/27/the-most-and-least-racially-diverse-u-s-religious-groups/

UUA (1997), "Toward an Anti-Racist Unitarian Universalist Association: 1997 Business Resolution," https://www.uua.org/action/statements/toward-anti-racist-unitarian-universalist-association

UUA (2020), "UUA Membership Statistics, 1961-2020," https://www.uua.org/data/demographics/uua-statistics

UU World (2010), "Racial and Ethnic Diversity of Unitarian Universalists," https://www.uuworld.org/articles/racial-ethnic-diversity-uus

WSUU (2018), "Beloved Congregations," https://wsuu.org/2018/11/07/sign-up-for-beloved-conversations-groups/

4 There Is No One Answer to What to Do

As far as diversity goes, there are no objectively correct or simple answers about what should be achieved and how to achieve it. There is no objective or correct answer as to how to organize a church or congregation and what should be its philosophy, purpose, or focus. Even a church focused on creating diversity has other major focuses and goals. (Aikin 2022)

Some UUs focus on doing whatever it takes to meet racial and ethnic quotas. Others say the object should instead be to be welcoming to those minorities who are attracted to UU's beliefs.

Some UUs are not troubled by the lack of racial diversity. They say that most churches and congregations have particular cultures and demographics, such as Scandinavian Lutheran and Eastern Orthodox congregations, many Muslim and Hindu temples, and Jewish synagogues. The least racially diverse American church is the National Baptist Convention with 99 percent black membership. Of the six least racially diverse American churches, three are 90+ percent white and the other three are either 90+ percent black or 90+ percent Asian. (Pew Research Center 2015)

For many of all races and ethnicities, the culture, demographic, traditional style of services, and music are what appeal to them. Further, a congregation mainly attracts people from its area, so will tend to reflect the neighborhood's demographics.

There is more than one way to skin a cat. Congregations can do interfaith work with other congregations and organizations. The UU congregation and synagogue I attend belong to an interfaith network with members from the neighborhood mosque, Hispanic Catholic congregation, Church of Latter-Day Saints, and other groups working together in local charity work. This type of work involves not only a diversity of races but of cultures and beliefs.

I belong to different communities. These include a mostly white but gender-diverse UU congregation, a mostly Ashkenazi synagogue, a racially and culturally diverse workplace, my multi-ethic extended family, and a vintage baseball card collecting club that is nearly all white male but with a wide diversity of religious and political beliefs. The combination of these and other relationships is my multi-cultural experience, and I neither expect nor want them all to be the same.

Multiculturalism

Many organizations including UU hold up the word "multiculturalism" as desirable or as a goal. True multiculturalism would involve not just a diversity of races, ethnicities, nationalities, and genders, but a diversity of often conflicting political, social, and religious views, values, and behaviors. Except for possibly a debate club, every organization and church have limits for what is accepted diversity and inclusion.

A self-proclaimed multicultural Christian church strives for the inclusion of different races, but not of Muslims, Hindus, and atheists. UU has limits, with UUs often expecting members to abide by its principles and values. While UU is pluralistic, an expressed Nazi, Stalinist, or homophobe would be asked to leave, and a Christian Evangelical, Calvinist, or Orthodox Jew would not fit.

There isn't one working definition of multiculturalism, diversity, or inclusion. Even in academic theory, there are different types of multiculturalism. These include the "melting pot" theory (assimilation) versus the "salad bowl" theory. New York City exemplifies the salad bowl with its many side-by-side ethnic communities, such as Little Odessa, Little Italy, and Chinatown. My described multicultural experience is salad bowl multiculturalism. (Longley 2020)

Within UU there are different approaches. There are attempts at general inclusion and representation. There are also identity groups, including services and programs for racial minorities only, LGBT+ only picnics, men's groups, and women's groups. There is talk of forming racial-minority-only congregations. UU attempts an uneasy combination of the melting pot and salad bowl.

The challenge of creating racial diversity and how to attract and maintain minorities in dominant white churches is not an issue just for Unitarian Unitarianism. There have been numerous attempts to create multi-racial Christian churches with challenges, successes, and failures. (Gjelten 2020)

References

Aikin J (2022), "I vs. We", Appendix

Gjelten, T. (2020), "Multiracial Congregations May Not Bridge Racial Divide," https://www.npr.org/2020/07/17/891600067/multiracial-congregations-may-not-bridge-racial-divide

Longley, R. (2020), "What Is Multiculturalism? Definition, Theories, and Examples," https://www.thoughtco.com/what-is-multiculturalism-4689285

5 Recent Radical Attempts at Change in UU and the Introduction of Critical Race Theory

In recent years the Unitarian Universalist Association (UUA) has been taken over by self-described radicals who, in the name of inclusion and diversity and to address dwindling membership, wish to make extreme, fundamental changes to UU. Their approach to the lack of racial diversity and shrinking membership is authoritarian, illiberal, and dogmatic, and rejects liberalism. (UU World 2021) (Schneider 2019) (Frederick-Gray 2021) (CLFUU 2017) (McCardle 2022)

The antiracism, anti-oppression approach national UU and UU groups have adopted is a fundamentalist, authoritarian form of critical race theory (CRT) incorporating the ideas of Ibram X. Kendi, author of *How to Be an Anti-Racist*, and Robin DiAngelo, author of *White Fragility*. *White Fragility* is published by the UUA's publisher, Beacon Press. Kendi and DiAngelo aren't critical race theorists but are influenced by CRT and have influenced many critical race theorists.

What Is Critical Race Theory (CRT)?

Critical race theory is a wide body of academic work designed to examine and address racial inequalities in society by manipulating racial groups and social structures. It is a postmodernist neo-Marxist ideology that focuses on races instead of classes. It is an application of critical theory, which was developed by a group of German Marxist scholars called the Frankfurt School. Critical theory has been applied not just to race but to many areas, including gender and disabilities. (Galston 2021) (Cole 2019) (Nickerson 2020)

Critical race theory was originally an American law school tool used to identify racial inequities in laws, such as inequities in drug sentencing. Its ideas have been applied more broadly, including in American society, institutions, and schools. (Smith 2020)

There are variations and different interpretations of and focuses within CRT, with the Unitarian Universalist Association (UUA) adopting an extreme version incorporating the ideas of Kendi and DiAngelo. (Kendi 2019)

The following are key ideas of critical race theory (CRT):

Critical race theory is a macro, not a micro view of society

CRT looks at society only at the large level, not at the personal level. CRT categorizes people in racial groups and doesn't consider people as unique individuals.

This is not to say adherents of CRT do not see people as individuals or that they say interpersonal one-to-one relations are unimportant. However, CRT does not look at people or society that way. It asserts that the ills of society can be solved only by large-scale manipulation of generic racial and other groups.

CRT says that race is a social construct, not a biological construct

CRT says that race is not objective, inherent, or fixed and that categories have been invented and manipulated to create and uphold power. For example, it says that whites created the racial categories of white and black to justify American slavery, Jim Crow laws, and segregation.

CRT proposes that racism is an ordinary, constant experience of racial minorities

According to CRT, due to the way American society and culture were constructed, racism is the normal way society does business and is the common experience of racial minorities. Robin DiAngelo says, "White identity is inherently racist." In *Critical Race Theory: An Introduction,* law professors Richard Delgado and Jean Stefancic write, "Many critical race theorists and social scientists alike hold that racism is pervasive, systemic, and deeply ingrained. If we take this perspective, then no white member of society seems quite so innocent." (DiAngelo 2019) (Delgado and Stefancic 2018) (Houchins 2022)

CRT feels that Western civilization and culture are inherently oppressive and should be dismantled

The genesis of CRT is that it sees that racial disparities persist in the post-civil rights era, which to it means that racism is inherent in the Western and American systems and culture themselves. Harvard civil rights law professor and CRT pioneer Derrick Bell wrote, "It appears that my worst fears have been realized: we have made progress in everything yet nothing has changed," and that "racism is so deeply rooted in the makeup of American society has beemas been able to reassert itself after each successive wave of reform aimed at eliminating it."

CRT feels that the whole system and culture was set up to uphold white privilege over racial minorities. It asserts the system cannot be fixed and must be dismantled. (George 2021) (Delgado and Stefancic 2017) (Lock 2021) (Gordon 2019)

CRT is not a liberal or progressive ideology

Many people wrongly associate critical race theory with liberalism (both the classical and American/Democratic Party versions) and progressivism. CRT is radical, and opposes liberalism and progressivism.

CRT sets up all of society and its peoples in a binary oppressor-versus-oppressed model

According to CRT and the theory of intersectionality, you are either a victim or an oppressor in society based on your race. Due to their inherent privilege, whites are oppressors, while blacks are inherently oppressed. Certain non-white groups that are deemed privileged are categorized as "white adjacent." These can include Ashkenazi Jews and Asian and Latin groups. In the theory of intersectionality, other demographics (gender, sexuality, disability, etc.) are similarly assigned to an oppressor versus victim socio-political-economic model. (Kuo 2018) (Aguilar 2017)

Critical race theory views American history through this lens. Critical race theorists argue that the United States of America was founded on racism, slavery, and white privilege and remains a fundamentally racist nation. The 1619 Project states that the United States was not founded in 1776 with the signing of the

Declaration of Independence, but by the arrival of the first slaves in 1619. (Wikipedia 2021) (Southern Poverty Law Center)

CRT is postmodernist

Critical race theory is postmodernist and uses postmodernist theories of knowledge and truth.

Postmodernists believe there is no knowable objective reality, and there is no certain or objective knowledge. Postmodernism does not believe there is historical or scientific objective truth. It is skeptical of science, technology, reason, humanism, mathematics, and logic. It does not believe those things lead to human progress, and believes that they have been used to create and maintain power and oppress minorities. It does not believe that reason and logic are universally valid, and believes that no general theory of the physical or social world is valid or true. It believes that different perspectives, such as science versus personal storytelling, are equally valid. (Pluckrose 2020) (Kuntz 2012) (Blummer 2022)

CRT wants to dismantle Western enlightenment, culture, and institutions

CRT is critical of the Western Enlightenment, classical liberalism, reason, the concept of objectivity, judicial equality, individualism, humanism, science, and the free market. It asserts that these things were designed, corrupted, and/or used to keep the dominant peoples in power. Critical race theorists believe that American institutions such as the Constitution, the Bill of Rights, and the legal system were made and are used to uphold white dominance. (Delgado and Stefancic 2018) (New Discourses 2019) (Lindsey 2021) (Blummer 2022)

As CRT is postmodernist, CRT narratives don't attempt to be objective, but instead to tell things that serve its purpose, including subverting traditional cultural norms and stories. Thus, the 1619 Project is not intended to be a full or objective telling of American history. (Harris 2020)

CRT believes that methods can be judged only by how they serve the final purpose. It rejects critiques of CRT based on reason, logic, science, and other "Western" methods of thinking. CRT regularly characterizes the use of logic, reason, critical thinking, and the scientific method to examine or critique CRT as "white" and "oppressive." CRT dogmatists dismiss any questioning or criticism as illegitimate, racist, and "white fragility."

CRT asserts that whites will only support change when it is in their interest

CRT believes in the restriction of freedom of speech and expression

Kendi, DiAngelo, and others say free speech supports the dominant views. A tenet of CRT is that platforming the dominant views drowns out and harms marginalized voices. Fundamentalist followers of CRT regularly try to silence dissenting and questioning views, and even punish dissenters. Robin DiAngelo categorizes any disagreement or questioning of what she teaches as "white fragility" that "upholds white supremacy." (Kendi 2015)

In the *First Amendment Encyclopedia*, Professor Chris Demaske writes, "In general, (CRT) scholars argue that there is no societal value in protecting speech that targets already oppressed groups. They also question the logic of using the First Amendment to protect speech that not only has no social value but also is socially and psychologically damaging to minority groups." (Demaske 2020)

As CRT considers the entire dominant American system and culture to be inherently racist, it believes that any support or participation in the systems, and even being neutral about the system, is racist

As it proposes that the system perpetuates racial disparities, CRT asserts that anyone who contributes or participates in the system upholds racism and patriarchy. This is why some say that, by being inescapably privileged in the system, whites are inherently racist. Kendi says that you are either an antiracist or a racist, and that being neutral or "not racist" is racist.

CRT upholds equity instead of equality

Equality means equal treatment of all.

As it asserts that the whole system is structurally biased against racial minorities, CRT says that equal treatment, color blindness, and meritocracy perpetuate the racist system and are racist. If a standardized test has racial disparity in outcome or a college science school has racial disparity, CRT says the test and school are racist. Any disparity is explained as racism.

As opposed to equality, equity means doing things to create equal outcomes. This includes discrimination against people due to their race and ethnicity, hiring quotas, removing standardized tests, and implementing affirmative action in universities. Kendi says the only remedy to racist discrimination is "antiracist discrimination," that the only remedy to past discrimination is present discrimination, and the only remedy to present discrimination is future discrimination.

Equality is creating equal opportunities, while equity means having equal outcomes. CRT focuses on outcomes. Under CRT, people are treated unequally.

CRT asserts that there is a monolithic, ubiquitous white culture

Based on the writing of activist Tema Okun, CRT claims that many qualities are monolithic to white culture and uphold white power in society. These qualities include the value of hard work, punctuality, worship of the written word, valuing ownership of goods and land, perfectionism, binary thinking, individualism, urgency, power hoarding, objectivity, defensiveness, and a belief that there is only one right way of doing things. Robert's Rules, science, logic, mathematics, and rationality are often categorized as "white ways of thinking." (McClone 2020) (City of Madison 2020)

Dalhousie University social justice theorist Raluca Bejan writes: "DiAngelo takes whiteness to be homogeneous. Phrases like 'white collective,' 'white dynamic,' 'white voice,' 'white frame of reference,' 'white worldview,' and 'white experience' are all used to suggest a certain racial sameness." (Bejan 2020)

CRT says only racial minorities can accurately talk about race and race issues

CRT gives privileged status to the voices of racial minorities and assigns lower status to white voices. It believes minority status brings with it a competence to speak about race and racism, while being white has an innate incompetence and ignorance on the topic. It believes that the majority can never truly understand the minority experience. Robin DiAngelo says, "To be white is to be functionally illiterate about race."

CRT believes in minorities' personal subjective experience, or 'lived experience,' as truth

According to CRT, as racial minorities have the presumed competence to speak about race and racism, their lived experiences and subjective perceptions take epistemological precedence over outside objective facts or views from culturally dominant people. Remember that objectivity, logic, and science are viewed skeptically as they are deemed "white ways of thinking" that are used to uphold the oppressive system. As a way of upending the dominant narrative, the subjective personal perceptions and stories of the minority are to be accepted and not questioned by whites.

CRT reinforces race and racial groups

Previous American civil rights movements believed in de-emphasizing racial categories and prejudices, striving for equality, and hoping for a colorblind society. CRT is opposed to this, as it believes that such an approach has not solved racial discrepancies. CRT is identitarian and reinforces racial groups and perceived inherent differences between the groups. Its intent is to manipulate these wholescale groups to bring about equality or equity. This is why it is neo-Marxist, focusing on racial instead of economic classes.

Terms associated with CRT and its antiracism approach:

Critical race theory and CRT-informed antiracism have a variety of terms, often redefining commonly used terms. Even when the term critical race theory is not used, the use of the following and other words imply CRT as an ideological framework: diversity, equity, and inclusion (DEI), antiracism, white supremacy culture, dismantling white supremacy, white fragility, whiteness, BIPOC, Latinx, colonizers, intersectionality. (Heritage Foundation 2020)

The following are some key terms and how they are defined by CRT:

Racism/racist

CRT has a different than commonly used definition.

In common usage, racism means personally believing one race is better than another. It means racial prejudice, hatred, or discrimination.

In CRT, racism means systemic or institutional racism. People don't have to have personal prejudice to participate in and uphold that system. The mere act of working to uphold the system, including by following norms of the dominant culture, is considered racist.

Antiracism

According to CRT, antiracism is doing things to help dismantle the system or to help make changes to racial equity.

According to Kendi, a person or political policy is either antiracist or racist. As he considers the system itself racist, he believes that even being neutral or calling oneself "not racist" is racist.

White supremacy/white supremacy culture

Despite its common association with the KKK and neo-Nazis, CRT defines white supremacy as all of white and dominant culture. CRT believes the whole of contemporary structure and culture keep whites in power over others. Such things as liberalism, logic, freedom of speech, critical thinking, mathematics, and Robert's Rules of Order are seen as part of white supremacy culture or "whiteness."

References

Aguilar, A. (2017), "Intersectionality of Privilege, Oppression, and Tactics of Abuse," https://www.cpedv.org/post/intersectionality-privilege-oppression-and-tactics-abuse

Bejan, R. (2020), "Robin DiAngelo's 'White Fragility' ignores the differences within whiteness," https://theconversation.com/robin-diangelos-white-fragility-ignores-the-differences-within-whiteness-143728

Blummer, R. (2022), "Identitarianism Is Incompatible with Humanism," https://secularhumanism.org/2022/05/identitarianism-is-incompatible-with-humanism/

City of Madison, WI (2021), "White Culture," https://www.cityofmadison.com/civil-rights/documents/RESJI_Part_3_prework.pdf

Cole, N. (2019), "The Frankfurt School of Critical Theory," https://www.thoughtco.com/frankfurt-school-3026079

Delgado and Stefancic (2107), *Critical Race Theory: An Introduction*, NYU Press

Demaske, C. (2020), "Critical Race Theory," https://www.mtsu.edu/first-amendment/article/1254/critical-race-theory

DiAngelo, R. (2019), "Robin DiAngelo: Debunking The Most Common Myths White People Tell About Race," https://www.youtube.com/watch?v=pO8qdwggIdI

Frederick-Gray, S. (2021), "Sea Change, Not Slow Change," https://www.uuworld.org/articles/president-fall-2021

Galston, W. (2021), "A Deeper Look at Critical Race Theory: The neo-Marxist movement rejects equal opportunity, merit, and objectivity," https://www.wsj.com/articles/kimberle-crenshaw-critical-race-theory-woke-marxism-education-11626793272

George, J. (2021), "A Lesson on Critical Race Theory," https://www.americanbar.org/groups/crsj/publications/human_rights_magazine_home/civil-rights-reimagining-policing/a-lesson-on-critical-race-theory/

Gordon, L. (2019), "Philosophical Methodologies of Critical Race Theory," https://blog.apaonline.org/2019/08/20/philosophical-methodologies-of-critical-race-theory/

Harris, L. (2020), "I Helped Fact-Check the 1619 Project. The Times Ignored Me," https://www.politico.com/news/magazine/2020/03/06/1619-project-new-york-times-mistake-122248

Kendi, I. (2015), "When Free Speech Becomes Unfree Speech," https://www.diverseeducation.com/students/article/15097335/when-free-speech-becomes-unfree-speech

Kendi, I. (2019), "How To Be An Antiracist by Ibram X. Kendi," https://www.youtube.com/watch?v=_OXMgA0Fwsk

Kuntz, M. (2012),"The postmodern assault on science: If all truths are equal, who cares what science has to say?", https://www.ncbi.nlm.nih.gov/pmc/articles/PMC3463968/

Kuo, I. (2018), "The 'Whitening' of Asian Americans," https://www.theatlantic.com/education/archive/2018/08/the-whitening-of-asian-americans/563336/

Lindsey, J. (2021) "What Is Critical Race Theory?", https://newdiscourses.com/2021/01/what-is-critical-race-theory/?

Locke (2021), "Where did critical race theory come from?", https://www.johnlocke.org/where-did-critical-race-theory-come-from/

McCardle, E. (2022), "Change from the Inside Out," https://www.uuworld.org/articles/change-inside

New Discourses (2019), "Critical Race Theory," https://newdiscourses.com/tftw-critical-race-theory/

Nickerson, C. (2022), "Understanding Critical Theory," https://www.simplypsychology.org/critical-theory.html

Pluckrose, H. (2020), "How French 'Intellectuals' Ruined the West: Postmodernism & Its Impact," https://newdiscourses.com/2020/04/french-intellectuals-ruined-west-postmodernism-impact/

Schneider, A. (2019), *The Self-Confessed "White Supremacy Culture": The Emergence of an Illiberal Left in Unitarian Universalism*, ISBN-10: 1692310283

Smith, E. (2020), "When anti-racism is just more racism: Yes, a form of CRT is being taught in schools," https://www.ydr.com/story/opinion/2021/10/21/yes-form-crt-being-taught-our-schools-opinion/6116736001/

Southern Poverty Law Center (2018), "Slavery shaped America's pathology on race and whiteness," https://www.splcenter.org/news/2019/08/17/weekend-read-slavery-shaped-americas-pathology-race-and-whiteness

Starr King Seminary (2017), "Critical Theory for Leaders," https://www.sksm.edu/course/critical-theory-for-leaders/

UU World (2019), "Why are we talking about white supremacy?", https://www.uuworld.org/articles/idiots-guide-critical-race-theory

UUC (2018), "More from Robin DiAngelo," https://www.uuchurch.org/2018/more-from-robin-diangelo/

Wikipedia (2021), "The 1619 Project," https://en.wikipedia.org/wiki/The_1619_Project

6 Positive Aspects of CRT

While I am a critic of critical race theory, I believe it offers important points and insights. I often agree with its basic ideas, but disagree with how CRT, or dogmatic CRT activists, wish to address or make use of the ideas. The following are examples of agreement.

- Despite great progress over the years, racial and other demographic disparities still exist in the American economy, society, and education. The sometimes contentious debates in the country, including within the minority groups, are about why these disparities exist and how they should be addressed, not about whether they exist.

- CRT is correct that American race categories are largely social and political rather than a biological construct, and that they have been used to discriminate against racial minorities. (Onwuachi-Willis 2016)

- All humans have unconscious biases toward different people, and these biases appear in institutions and structures. We all must work on being aware of, overcoming, and compensating for our biases. I agree that structures and methods should be altered to make things fair, for example making sure job interviewers don't unconsciously tend to pick people who are like them, and making sure tests aren't unduly culturally biased.

- American standard history books have been white-centric and patriarchal. When I look at my 1978 *New World Encyclopedia*, I see its clear bias in subjects, descriptions, and language. American society and institutions must become more diverse. The majority should listen to minority perspectives, and history books must reflect the diversity of experiences.

- As a philosopher and cognitive scientist I know that there is no known objective truth, and that humans can only view the world from their personal perspectives. Though not practically workable in the real world, the postmodernist philosophy of knowledge is technically true.

- While I support liberalism, freedom of speech, and democracy, I know they are imperfect and often must be checked. For example, straight democracy can lead to tyranny of the majority. While I support freedom of expression and speech, I'm not an absolutist and know the majority must make space for minority and heterodox ideas.

- All countries and societies have dominant cultures. Dominant cultures must accommodate and empower different cultures. Part of my research and writing is in neurodiversity and studying people whose brains function differently. People with mental disorders such as ADHD, dyslexia, and autism have trouble fitting in with the dominant culture. Society must learn to appreciate and accommodate such different thinkers, both for the individual's and for society's benefit. Societies need heterodoxy and diversity. (Bernstein 2022)

- Science, logic, and reason are invaluable ways of thinking. However, CRT is correct that there are other important ways of thinking. Areas such as morality, ethics, art, and spirituality are beyond the scope of science and logic. Science and logic aren't the arbiter of all things. It is also true that academic philosophy and science in practice have had a history of biases against minorities. I support CRT's idea of including different ways of thinking and ridding science and other academic areas of racism, sexism, and other bigotry. (Oreskes 2020)

References

Bernstein, D. (2022), "In Search of Systemic Racism," https://freeblackthought.substack.com/p/in-search-of-systemic-racism

Oreskes, N. (2020), "Racism and Sexism in Science Haven't Disappeared," https://www.scientificamerican.com/article/racism-and-sexism-in-science-havent-disappeared/

Onwuachi-Willis (2016), "Race and Racial Identity Are Social Constructs," https://www.nytimes.com/roomfordebate/2015/06/16/how-fluid-is-racial-identity/race-and-racial-identity-are-social-constructs

7 Common Criticisms of Critical Race Theory

As described in the next chapter, critical race theory (CRT) is a large and diverse body of work and is considered and used in different ways. The focus in this chapter is on what happens when people dogmatically use CRT as the overriding lens for everything. Kendi's and DiAngelo's ideas are examples of such dogmatism and fundamentalism. Whether or not they are critical race theorists and because the UUA relies so much on them, I include them in the mix.

The following offers many standard criticisms of CRT.

All knowledge is provisional, and all dogma is necessarily wrong

It is the evangelical dogmatism and intolerance of any dissent of many CRT adherents that turn off so many people, including people within the political left. Folks such as Kendi and DiAngelo present their views as dogma, saying that any disagreement with the views is wrong and racist. For example, Kendi says, "In order to truly be anti-racist, you also have to truly be anti-capitalist." He is thus saying that any minorities who support or participate in capitalism are racist.

The use of ad hominem arguments, the dismissal of any criticism or dissent as "racist" and "white fragility," and saying only certain people can express views on the matter, is intellectually authoritarian and unacceptable.

The irony of CRT fundamentalists is when they say there is no objective knowledge or known objectively true model but present their ideology as dogma.

CRT is reductionist, and no model can explain everything

No model can encompass the whole of society and oppression. CRT is too simplistic. As with any model, there are areas outside of its domain and there are experiences that counter it.

Many argue that class must be part of the equation or even the primary lens, including in areas such as affirmative action, law, and structural changes. For example, many feel that affirmative action for student entry into universities should be based on class, not race. (Kahlenberg 2018) (Rubin 2018) (Moss 2003)

Academics Glenn Loury at Brown University, John McWhorter at Columbia University, Thomas Sowell at Stanford, and Michael Creswell at Florida State University say that disparities in outcomes are often due to more than just present racism, pointing to cultural differences and other historical factors. (McWhorter 2020) (Sowell 2005) (Knight-Laurie 2022) (Creswell 2022)

A counter to CRT's binary oppressor versus victim model are the minority groups that have succeeded under the system and whites who have not. Despite the claim that the system is being set up against all non-whites, many Jews, Asians, Indians, Latinos, Africans, and Caribbeans have succeeded in the system. The average Indian-American household income is higher than that of whites, the median income of Asian women is higher than that of white men, and two-thirds of blacks in Ivy League schools are second-generation Nigerians and Caribbeans. (Pew

2012) (Jilani, Wilcox and Wang 2021) (Joseph 2021) (Economic Times 2021) (Raleigh 2021) (Loury 2022)

Chinese-born American Helen Raleigh writes, "According to CRT's victimization ledger, all whites are oppressors, and all 'people of color' are oppressed. CRT argues that unequal economic outcomes among different races in our society result from white power and white privilege. Asian Americans punch a big hole in that worldview. As a group, their economic achievement has surpassed that of all other racial groups, including whites." (Raleigh 2021)

There also are groups of whites who are poor and socially immobile over generations despite CRT saying they have an inherent advantage.

Stanford law professor Randall Ralph Richard Banks says that many things are going on in society and that "[f]ocusing only on race is a mistake. Once you start to divide society into the oppressor and the oppressed and the black people are always on the downside and the white people are always the possessors of privilege, I think that's a mistake. It's a mistake to fixate on the idea of white privilege because most white people in American society are not and don't feel themselves to be privileged. Most white people in American society are actually struggling. They're struggling to raise their children. They worry about whether their children's lives will be better than their own. They confront all manner of illness and distress and economic anxiety. So it's both analytically wrong and politically misguided to promote an ideology that suggests that all white people have it good and all black people have it bad." (Manhattan Institute 2021)

Arizona State University political science professor and author of *(Dis)Continuing Racial Inequality: Essays on Race in the U.S.* Anne Schneider challenges critical race theory's central premise "that there is a homogeneous, hegemonic white culture, and that everything in it benefits white people and disadvantages POC. Instead, I make an argument for culture as a mosaic, with many different threads running through it." (Schneider 2019)

Many mistake the privilege and social power of the tiny number of highest-class whites for that of all whites. UU minister Rev. Thandeka said there is "the errant assumption that white America works for white Americans. Anyone who cares to look will quickly discover that it doesn't—at least, not for the vast majority of them. The privilege that, according to the anti-racists, comes with membership in white America, actually belongs to a tiny elite." (Thandeka 2009)

The whole postmodernist view is untenable

The whole rejection of logic, science, and reason, along with dismissing the use of logic, reason, and the scientific method in examining and critiquing CRT, is untenable and dysfunctional in real-world situations. This makes CRT akin to religious dogma. Extremists on the left who reject facts and critical thinking are as bad as Trump supporters and their "alternative facts."

Philosopher Saul Sorrell-Till writes, "How exactly do these people think they construct their arguments if not by logic and reason? You literally cannot communicate with another human being without those tools. It's like saying we should try breathing without air."

Society and the world are in grave trouble when logic, reason, and the scientific method are disregarded. Rejection of science and lack of critical thinking exists in both the right and left. Anti-science in the far right is commonly associated with creationism and climate change denial. Areas of anti-science in the far left include being anti-GMO or anti-nuclear and rejecting scientific knowledge that conflicts with postmodernist social justice ideologies. (Salzberg 2016) (Pearce 2012) (Shermer 2013)

French scientist Michel Kuntz writes, "Postmodernist thought is being used to attack the scientific worldview and undermine scientific truths; a disturbing trend that has gone unnoticed by a majority of scientists." Harvard psychology professor Steven Pinker writes that postmodernism threatens science by questioning the possibility of objective truth. (Kuntz 2012) (Illing 2019) (Goldhill 2018) (Soh 2017) (Shermer (2013) (Tucker 2021)

Critical race theory is an ideology, not a theory

Despite its name, critical race theory is not a theory but an ideology. Theories must be falsifiable, meaning empirically testable, and CRT is not. CRT begs questions and uses circular logic. It presents unproven assertions that are expected to just be accepted. (Losada 2020) (Church 2010)

University of Illinois at Urbana-Champaign associate professor of sociology Ilana Redstone writes, "The problem is that CRT and its related ideas form a closed system. It's a perspective that leaves no space for anyone, no matter how well-intentioned, to see the world differently. When presented as the singular valid worldview, it isn't a productive way to engage with students, [with] groups, or with one another." (Redstone 2018)

Economist Jonathan Church writes, "Unfortunately, in so blithely dismissing individualism, DiAngelo hinges her theory so heavily on collective, rather than individual, identity and experience that it dies on the sword of a logical fallacy," and "[When Kendi] sees racial disparities, he sees racism. As nature abhors a vacuum, Kendi abhors any analysis of racial inequality that 'racism' cannot explain. This reflexive mono-causality gives us a basic logical fallacy in Kendi's work: the fallacy of affirming the consequent." (Church 2019) (Church 2020)

In *Why Ibram Kendi's Antiracism Is So Flawed,* Carleton College education studies professor Jeffrey Aaron Snyder writes, "Kendi offers up a tantalizing promise that has proven highly seductive for many Americans who are waking up to the realities of racial injustice. It is a choose-your-own-adventure where you always have just two options: racist or antiracist. This either-or paradigm, alas, presents a highly misleading picture of the nature and consequences of ideas, policies, and social movements. It describes a world that never was and never will be—a world without contradictions, ironies, or unintended consequences." (Snyder 2021)

Unitarian Universalists for a Just Economic Community (UUJEC) inequality expert Dick Burkhart wrote, "CRT is not grounded in the social sciences, but is a collection of ideologies, often characterized by speculation, prejudice, and sophistry, growing out of the subjectivity of postmodern philosophy."

All models, theories, and ideologies must be examined and questioned. All have limits, problems, and blind spots. Honest theorists should invite critiques, as that's how theories and models are improved and corrected. (Pluckrose 2020) (McWhorter 2020) (Hughes 2020)

Nigerian-raised British politician and CRT-critic Kemi Badenoch said in a House of Commons speech, "What we are against is the teaching of contested political ideas as if they are accepted fact. We don't do this with communism, we don't do this with socialism, we don't do it with capitalism." (Badenoch 2020)

CRT antiracism can be authoritarian

Aspects of CRT and extreme antiracism ideology are about the dismantling of institutions and culture, skepticism of democracy, ending equal treatment in courts, and the suppression of freedom of speech and dissent. Ibram X. Kendi proposed the following constitutional amendment to create a Federal Department of Anti-Racism:

> "To fix the original sin of racism, Americans should pass an anti-racist amendment to the U.S. Constitution that enshrines two guiding anti-racist principles: Racial inequity is evidence of racist policy and the different racial groups are equals. The amendment would make unconstitutional racial inequity over a certain threshold, as well as racist ideas by public officials (with "racist ideas" and "public official" clearly defined). It would establish and permanently fund the Department of Anti-Racism (DOA) comprised of formally trained experts on racism and no political appointees. The DOA would be responsible for preclearing all local, state and federal public policies to ensure they won't yield racial inequity, monitor those policies, investigate private racist policies when racial inequity surfaces, and monitor public officials for expressions of racist ideas. The DOA would be empowered with disciplinary tools to wield over and against policymakers and public officials who do not voluntarily change their racist policy and ideas." (Kendi 2019)

Philosopher and social critic Coleman Hughes writes that "Kendi's goals are openly totalitarian. The DOA would be tasked with 'investigating' private businesses and 'monitoring' the speech of public officials; it would have the power to reject any local, state, or federal policy before it's implemented; it would be made up of 'experts' who could not be fired, even by the president; and it would wield 'disciplinary tools' over public officials who did not 'voluntarily' change their 'racist ideas'—as defined, presumably, by people like Kendi. What could possibly go wrong?" (Hughes 2019)

Much of the illiberalism, censorship, circular logic, dogmatism, and cancel culture associated with extreme social justice ideologues are because an ideology for changing the whole of society only works when the masses follow them. It is about obtaining power, not expressing truth.

Liberalism and Western Enlightenment ideals are important

The majority of Americans support Western Enlightenment ideals. They see liberalism as the best way to create a just world and long-lasting social and political progress. They support reason, logic, critical thinking, mathematics, and science as essential methods to come to understanding and knowledge. They fear recent movements in both the far left and far right towards illiberalism, authoritarianism, suppression of freedom of speech and individual rights, and skepticism of logic, reason, and democracy.

CRT points out legitimate problems in society, but its response to them is too extreme. The dismissal of objectivity, reason, legal equality, meritocracy, individualism, freedom of expression, and capitalism is throwing out the baby with the bathwater. (Pluckrose 2021)

Liberalism is imperfect and, as with all systems including science, must continually work to improve. It is true that the

United States originally offered equality, justice, democracy, and freedom of speech only to white men. The answer to such inequality and injustice is not to throw out these things, but to extend them to all Americans. That was the dream of Martin Luther King Jr. and Frederick Douglass.

CRT and the teachings of Kendi and DiAngelo divide rather than unite people, making them counterproductive to social justice

Whether or not you agree with them, CRT and Kendi's and DiAngelo's views are extreme, radical approaches that oppose the commonly held ideals of most Americans. These and other approaches are inherently controversial, fanning the flames of culture wars and tribalism and making dysfunctional communities. They cause division and strife even within the political left. This makes them counterproductive to social justice. (Cillizza 2021) (Lind 2020) (Zucher 2021) (Schlott 2020) (Thandeka 2009)

David L. Bernstein of the Institute for Liberal Values believes that "an ideological formula that prioritizes collective culpability over individual responsibility will only exacerbate racial tensions." Political science professor Anne Schneider writes, "We need a unifying strategy, not a divisive and segregated strategy; we need 'we' working together in multi-racial groups as advocates for justice." (Bernstein 2020) (Schneider 2019)

Religion and sociology professor emeritus and social justice activist Kenneth Christiansen writes that guilt-based techniques, such as labeling all whites racist and white supremacist, have a poor record of uniting people for social justice. He writes, "Persons who see themselves as assets that can bring about needed positive changes will accomplish much more for the common good than persons who are overwhelmed by feelings of guilt." (Christiansen 2020)

Racial stereotyping and racial essentialism are ignorant and racist

CRT accuses others of racism while standing behind a view predicated on race, racial stereotypes, and racial essentialism.

Defining any race, ethnicity, nationality, or large group as monolithically "all this" or "all that" is a simplistic and ignorant stereotyping that one would think antiracism would be aspiring to overcome. Racial essentialism is wrong whether it is by the far right or the far left.

The idea that whites are a monolithic group and have a single culture is clearly false. There is great diversity of cultures amongst whites. It's bizarre to claim that Scandinavians and Southern Italians or whites in the Bronx and rural Alabama share the same culture. (Bejan 2020)

The idea that blacks are one cultural group due to the color of their skin is ignorant. Glenn Loury doesn't capitalize the word black, because he says "blacks," "whites," "yellows" and "browns" simply aren't whole, monolithic groups. (Loury 2021)

Loury writes: "The term 'people of color' attempts to unite an extraordinarily diverse segment of Americans of many different racial and ethnic backgrounds, of different classes, and of different cultural predilections under a single umbrella. What is the justification for this? Some progressives will tell you that all 'people of color' share a common experience, which is that they have suffered the oppression of white supremacy or systemic racism. Even granting the existence of such universal oppression (which I do not), would it justify describing the experiences of, say, a newly arrived South Korean delivery driver and the second-generation child of Harvard-educated Bahamian lawyers as, in any meaningful way, 'the same'? Of course not. To group two such people together, you would have to ignore everything about them except the fact that they are not white." (Loury 2022)

The idea that mathematics, science, and logic are "white ways of thinking" is not only racist but ignorant about the history of these areas. For example, mathematical logic is not a product of the West. Africa, the Middle East, and Southeast Asia were integral to its development long before it ever reached Europe. Cambodia first used a symbol for zero, and the Western numeral system is Hindu-Arabic. (Loury & McWhorter 2021)

A white University of Chicago math professor said that he would be fired if he told students that math was "a white way, not a black way of thinking." Demonizing math and science economically hurts minorities in a world that vocationally values such areas.

In a sermon, a newly ordained Unitarian Universalist minister used the term "white science" and said that science was "white." I afterward wrote to him about how ignorant this statement and how racist such stereotyping were to racial minorities. The empirical method is a universal system. Indians, Japanese, Chinese, and Koreans are at the cutting edge of science and technology. The Middle East, Africa, and Latin America have rich histories in science. Over 22 percent of Nobel Prize winners were Jewish. Just a few years ago, one would expect to hear such statements coming only from a White Nationalist or a KKK member, not ever from a "progressive" UU minister.

Tema Okun's widely used "traits of white supremacy culture"-- hard work ethic, punctuality, perfectionism, individualism, urgency, objectivity, etc.— are unscientific, wrongly assume there is a monolithic white culture and have been widely criticized. Professor Schneider writes that the author offers no evidence ("not a single citation") to back up the assertions. Even Okun's list itself said, "This article was not the result of research." (Yglesias 2021)

Okun's theory ironically reinforces stereotypes against blacks and other racial minorities. Jerry Coyne wrote, "If they showed the opposite traits of those given above for Black Culture, it would look exceedingly racist," and called it "nonsense, a form of nonsense that seems not only distorted, misleading, but positively divisive. Is this kind of stuff going to heal racial divides? I doubt it." (Coyne 2020)

Criticizing the legitimacy of Okun's work, David L. Bernstein writes, "There is nothing inherently supremacist about valuing perfectionism or a sense of urgency or anything particularly egalitarian or enlightened about valuing their opposites— inattentiveness and laxity. What's more, these are by no means 'white cultural traits.' Many whites have a very low sense of urgency and many non-whites a high sense of urgency, for example." (Bernstein 2022)

John McWhorter has written that DiAngelo's ideas expressed in *White Fragility* are racist and harmful to blacks. He writes: "*White Fragility* is racist, and I don't mean that Robin DiAngelo is a racist. I'm not calling her that. But I'm saying that if you write a book that teaches that Black people's feelings must be stepped around to an exquisitely sensitive degree that hasn't been required of any human beings, you're condescending to Black people. In supposing that Black people have no resilience, you are saying that Black people are unusually weak. You're saying that we are lesser. You're saying that we, because of the circumstances of American social history, cannot be treated as adults. And in the technical sense, that's discriminatory." (McWhorter 2020)

Canadian lawyer and Senior Fellow at the Macdonald-Laurier Institute Jamil Jivina writes that stereotypes about blacks by progressives are often as ignorant and harmful as stereotypes by the right. He writes that "Black thought has always been inconveniently free," and, "Today, some of the stereotypes that harshly impact black communities are rooted in progressive politics. Television, radio, and newspapers offensively caricature black people as anti-police, dependent on big government programs, consumed by historical grievances, accepting of immoral pop culture, incompatible with traditional nuclear family values, and unpatriotic. Across North America, liberal stereotypes have real consequences. Stereotypes of all varieties cloud one's ability to see nuance." (Jivani 2022)

CRT's categorization of successful Asians, light-skinned Jews, and Hispanics as white or "white adjacent" is ignorant and offensive to many in those groups. Asian-Americans were outraged when the North Thurston (WA) Public Schools said that Asians weren't racial minorities and grouped them with whites because they did well on tests. (Northwest Asian Weekly) (Kuo 2018) (Lerner 1993) (JILV 2021) (Coyne 2021) (Paresky 2021) (Dunst 2020)

Kenny Xu of the Foundation Against Intolerance and Racism (FAIR) and author of the book *An Inconvenient Minority: The Attack on Asian American Excellence and the Fight for Meritocracy*, writes, "Asian Americans are not 'white-adjacent.' They are unique individuals from many distinct cultures. Their individual successes are theirs alone, and belittling those successes as 'white-adjacent' is racist in myriad ways." (Xu 2021)

Chinese American author Patricia Pan Connor writes, "Calling Asians 'White Adjacent' is racist and insulting. The idea that Asian Americans are too successful to be persons of color assumes success is a 'white' trait." (Connor 2021)

As described in Chapter 14, the American categorizing of Jews as "white" and part of the "white supremacy" is offensive to many Jews, with the Jewish Institute for Liberal Values saying that CRT "erases Jewish identity." (JILV 2021)

Extreme CRT narratives give a distorted, blinkered view of the United States and U.S. history

As with any country, the United States and its history have good and bad aspects, great achievements and dark chapters. U.S. history is about democracy and free press, great scientific and technological achievements, religious freedom, the Declaration of Independence, and the Constitution. It is also about mistreatment of Indians, slavery, and racial segregation and the ills of unbridled capitalism. As with all humans, the traditional history-book heroes such as George Washington, Thomas Jefferson, and Franklin Delano Roosevelt were multi-faceted and flawed human beings. The country's heroes and chapters were products of their time, as we are of ours.

Traditional American history books depicting U.S. history as entirely glorious and viewing it through a narrow white patriarchal lens have been myopic and minimized or ignored many bad aspects. A truer history must give the perspectives and experiences of other peoples, including women, American Indians, racial minorities, and non-Americans.

While still imperfect, the current United States has made great strides in racial justice and women's rights. It ranks high among the countries with the most racial and ethnic diversity, religious and political freedom, and minority rights. Racial minorities, gays, lesbians and trans people are now commonly shown in television shows, commercials, and movies. Blacks have been President, Vice-President, and Secretary of State. The Supreme Court has included blacks, Jews, women, and a Latina. Unlike in many other countries, people who complain loudly about the country are given the right to speak.

The United States has the most migrants, and is by far the most desired destination of migrants, including racial minority migrants. Irish immigrant Andrew Sullivan asked that if the United States is as entirely racist and socially and economically oppressive as some claim, then why do so many racial minorities choose to come here? My friend is Iranian and was an ethnic and religious minority both in her homeland and the United States. She said that in the Middle East, the United States was the most common desired location to immigrate to because it was well known as a place of opportunity for immigrants. (Citizenpath 2020) (Edmond 2017)

The more extreme adherents of critical race theory, however, paint the United States as overwhelmingly racist and oppressive and rotten to the core. They claim that US history can only accurately be viewed through the lens of slavery, racism, and oppression. Some claim there has been no improvement. Comedian Kevin Hart said that "white power and white privilege is at an all-time high." (Ortiz-Dunbar 2020)

Such a lens of the United States and history is as distorted and false as previous glorified, whitewashed views of American history. (Gasman 2021)

Harvard psychologist Steven Pinker coined the term "progressophobia," which is where leftist activists can't recognize or acknowledge progress. Political comedian Bill Maher jokingly defined it as "a brain disorder that strikes liberals" and said, "If you think America is more racist now than ever, more sexist than before women could vote, and more homophobic than when blow jobs were a felony, you have progressophobia and you should adjust your mask because it's covering your eyes." (Pinker 2018) (Maher 2020)

Jerry Coyne wrote, "I don't see why we can't fight to improve things at the same time we admit that they *have* improved. Who but a historical ignoramus could claim that the rights of people of color haven't improved in the last 75 years?" (Coyne 2020)

CRT is American-centric and thus myopic and eccentric. This is exemplified by those who promote the false ideas that the U.S. and the West invented slavery and that slavery was a product of racism. Alex Haley said that, with his novel *Roots,* he was "[t]rying to make a myth for my people to live by," and this narrative is how most Americans primarily see the whole of slavery.

Slavery was once a universal institution. It has existed for thousands of years all over the world, and nearly all peoples of all skin colors have been enslaved at some time. Until very recently in world history, slavery was not of other races. Europeans enslaved Europeans, Asians enslaved Asians, American Indians enslaved American Indians, and Africans enslaved and traded Africans. The word slavery comes from the word root "Slav," a word that refers to a north Euro-Asian ethnic group. (Sowell 2006) (Sowell 2010) (Perry 2017)

Stanford economist and historian Thomas Sowell writes: "Of all the tragic facts about the history of slavery, the most astonishing to an American today is that, although slavery was a worldwide institution for thousands of years, nowhere in the world was slavery a controversial issue prior to the 18th century. People of every race and color were enslaved—and enslaved others. White people were still being bought and sold as slaves in the Ottoman Empire, decades after American blacks were freed." (Sowell 2010)

Not only didn't the West invent slavery, but it was the West that moved to abolish it against the wishes of people in other parts of the world. The world's trade in slaves and then slavery itself was abolished by the British in the 19th century against opposition in Africa and Asia. Slavery still commonly exists, not in the West but in the East, Middle East, and Africa. The five countries with the most slaves are India, China, North Korea, Nigeria, and Iran. (WorldAtlas 2020) (Sowell 2010) (Perry 2017) (Reuters 2017)

Writes Sowell: "Everyone hated the idea of being a slave but few had any qualms about enslaving others. Slavery was just not an issue, not even among intellectuals, much less among political leaders, until the 18th century—and then it was an issue only in Western civilization. Among those who turned against slavery in the 18th century were George Washington, Thomas Jefferson, Patrick Henry, and other American leaders. You could research all of 18th century Africa or Asia or the Middle East without finding any comparable rejection of slavery there." (Sowell 2010) (Sowell in Perry 2017)

An honest history must be honest and whole. The 1619 Project, for example, offers an additional perspective on United States history but is as limited and distorted as previous white, patriarchal history books.

The American color-coded categories of race are eccentric, shallow, and different from the definitions used in most of the world.

Depending on the prevailing or political and ideological sentiments in the United States, Japanese, Latinos, Irish, Greeks, Ashkenazim, and Arabs have fallen in and out of the "white" category. Armenians have alternately been classified in the United States as "yellow," "white" and "brown." Though, if you ask Armenians, they usually will reject any color label, as that is not how they, and many other non-Westerners, define race. I attended a lecture on Islam by two Somali immigrants to the United States. One said they didn't like it when Americans called them black "because that's not how Somalis view people." (Arzoumanian 2020)

When Americans apply their American-centric racial views to other places in the world it has caused offense and shows how peculiar are American perceptions. An example is when some Americans call the Holocaust "white on white" violence and say, "The Holocaust wasn't about race." Law professor David E. Bernstein says this is not only ignorant but a sign of "intellectual moral decay." The Nazis classified and persecuted Jews as a different and inferior race. (Sowell 2021) (Bernstein 2016) (Bejan 2021)

The claim that one minority group over another has more knowledge of truth and that the perceptions of minorities cannot be questioned is irrational and bigoted

To disrupt the dominant narrative, CRT says the personal subjective perceptions of racial minorities must be accepted by the dominant culture. It is perceived as causing "harm" to question and to ask for evidence for the claims.

Uplifting different perspectives is important. However, the idea that anyone's emotional perception is objective and an unquestionable statement of truth clearly is false, in particular considering that different people of the same demographic have different perceptions. Psychologist Jonathan Haidt says that such emotional thinking "as proof" is cognitive distortion. (Seager 2018)

I am autistic and know that not only will other autistic people have different views than mine, but I can be wrong on autism topics and people without autism can have important perspectives and insights in the area.

I am Jewish and Jews have all sorts of views on any given topic, including Judaism and antisemitism. To treat my particular opinion on a Jewish topic as "unquestionable truth" is dumb, including to Jews. Some Jews will respond, "Certainly not! I disagree with what David says."

Harvard law professor Randall Kennedy said in a discussion about CRT: "And then there was a second argument that was being made, which was that minority people had a sort of special insight into certain areas of culture, certain areas of law. And I pushed back against that because I think that in the area of culture in the intellectual realm, we shouldn't be putting up racial fences." (Manhattan Institute 2021)

Bari Weiss says that it is wrong to say that "certain people have more hold of the truth and are more morally pure because of the amount of melanin in their skin." (Manhattan Institute 2021)

CRT holds up the subjective views and "lived experiences" of racial minorities only when they support CRT's ideology

CRT claims it holds up the "lived experiences" of racial minorities. However, in reality, it only holds up the lived experiences of minorities when those experiences support the narrative. Black conservatives Thomas Sowell and Shelby Steele have less credibility in the eyes of CRT proponents than white allies such as Robin DiAngelo or Peggy McIntosh. Racial minorities who do not subscribe to the ideology are said to have work on their "inner racism" and are said to not have an "authentic" minority voice. The hypocrisy is clear.

In the *Journal of Free Black Thought* essay "We Love Lived Experience . . . Until It Undermines the Narrative: Critical Justice Ideology Cannot Define Me," African immigrant Kimi Katiti writes that "[w]hen I identified as a victim, my lived experience was lauded by all as authentic. However, when I came out as a proudly free-thinking black individual, and no longer claimed victimhood as a part of my identity, my lived experience was rejected and discredited by both friends and strangers alike." (Katiti 2021)

The dogmatic and divisive focus on race entrenches racism

Seeing everything through the lens of race will not solve racism. It will exacerbate racism and racial strife. Harvard law professor Randall Kennedy says that many CRT adherents' belief that race is the sole factor in the ills of society creates a "danger of race narcissism." (Manhattan Institute 2021)

Social psychologist and mediator Tara West has written about how CRT will increase prejudice:

> So when I talk about CRT, I'm referring to a collection of practices that communicate the following assumptions: that race is a defining feature of a person's identity, that racism is pervasive, and that the color of one's skin determines whether a person is the oppressor or the oppressed. It's not all-or-nothing, but to the extent that these assumptions are communicated (especially to children), I think they're likely to increase rather than decrease prejudice.
>
> So telling people that members of racial groups are either the oppressors or the oppressed creates the perception that racial groups are in conflict over limited resources (e.g., power, social status, wealth, etc.), which should increase prejudice between groups.

Studies have shown that DiAngelo-style antiracism training not only doesn't work but makes things worse. Making training attendees focus on race often makes them more racist. Mandatory training also hasn't increased diversity and often decreases it. (Chait 2020) (Dobbin & Kalev 2016) (al-Gharbi 2020) (Bregman 2012)

In the 2016 *Harvard Business Review* report "Why Diversity Programs Fail," sociology professors Frank Dobbin of Harvard and Alexandra Kalev of Tel Aviv University write that "laboratory studies show that this kind of force-feeding can activate bias rather than stamp it out," and, "The numbers sum it up. Your organization will become less diverse, not more, if you require managers to go to diversity training, try to regulate their hiring and promotion decisions, and put in a legalistic grievance system." (Dobbin & Kalev)

In another *Harvard Business Review* article titled "Diversity Training Doesn't Work," executive coach Peter Bregman writes that the DiAngelo-style training has it backwards: "Rather than changing attitudes of prejudice and bias, it solidified them. . . . When people divide into categories to illustrate the idea of diversity, it reinforces the idea of the categories." (Bregman 2012)

Bregman says what does work is for workers to work with a diversity of people and learn to see them not as "dehumanizing" categories but as individual human beings: "The solution? Instead of seeing people as categories, we need to see people as people. Stop training people to be more accepting of diversity. It's too conceptual, and it doesn't work. Instead, train them to do their work with a diverse set of individuals. Not categories of people. People." (Bregman 2012)

State University of New York African American Literature professor Sheena Mason, libertarian Kmele Foster, and former black nationalist Reinard Knight-Laurie believe that the only way to overcome racism is to deemphasize race. Mason writes, "To eliminate racism we must eliminate race." Knight-Laurie writes, "True anti-racism means being anti-race." (Loury and McWhorter 2021) (Mason 2021) (Knight-Laurie 2021)

Director of Black Americans for Inclusive Ethnic Studies Brandy Shufutinsky is for a colorblind society, explaining: "Being colorblind doesn't mean you don't see someone's color. Of course, you see that I'm black and I want you to see that I'm black. I'm proud of being black. Colorblind means you don't do things or make choices based on someone's color." (JILV 2020)

CRT is a minority view of minorities

For any demographic there is no one voice, no one view, no one theory, no one language, no one way of looking at the world. Respecting any demographic is knowing and respecting that there is a wide variety of philosophies, views, political persuasions, language, and opinions in the group.

Disability, skin color, or gender isn't an ideology or a political position. Someone who advocates for wheelchair accessibility might be a progressive or a conservative. A saying about the autistic is, "If you've met one autistic person, you've met one autistic person." Educator Irshad Manji says, "Just because I'm gay, just because I'm Muslim, doesn't mean I think any particular way." Orthodox Rabbi Shaye Cohen said, "A secular atheist Jew such as Richard Feynman is just as Jewish as me." Expectations of ideological and political conformity are the antithesis of multiculturalism and diversity. (Manji 2019)

Erec Smith, professor of rhetoric at York College and co-editor of *Journal of Free Black Thought*, writes, "Black thought varies as widely as black individuals. There are black conservatives and liberals, socialists and free-marketeers, traditionalists and radicals, theists and atheists, everything in between, and more besides. *Free Black Thought* seeks to represent the rich diversity of black thought beyond the relatively narrow spectrum of views promoted by mainstream outlets as defining 'the black perspective.'" (Smith 2020)

John McWhorter says that the critical race theory is "not the general black view of things." Glenn Loury, the first tenured black American economics professor at Harvard, strongly objects when only a certain point of view amongst the great diversity of black thought is represented as the "authentic black voice." Saying that one black perspective is "authentic" and others' are not is a bogus, self-serving argument. Former Bernie Sanders National Press Secretary and podcaster Briahana Joy Gray says about her podcast discussions, "I always love to talk with heterodox voices across the political spectrum, particularly those that make it clear that there is not one Black voice." (McWhorter 2021) (Loury 2021) (Gray in Loury 2021)

In the *Journal of Free Black Thought*, educator and Democratic politician Barrington Martin II writes, "The conservative nature of black Americans is largely ignored both by the politicians they vote for and by the media. Although black turnout for Democrats is high, black people are less likely to identify as liberal than whites or Hispanics, are pro-gun ownership, are the most religious ethnic group in America, and favor school choice. Yet the media platforms only a narrow sampling of black authors, such as Nikole Hannah-Jones, Ta-Nehisi Coates, and Ibram X. Kendi, whose positions are antithetical to more widely-shared values." He feels that both parties have failed black America. (Martin 2022)

Some of the strongest objections to critical race theory and related ideas have come from racial and ethnic minorities such as McWhorter, Loury, Ayan Hirsi Ali, Inaya Folarin Iman, Zaid Jilani, Wilfred Reilly, Wenyan Wu, Thomas Chatterton Williams, Thomas Sowell, Irshad Manji, Bari Weiss, Pamela Paresky, Shelby Steele, Kenny Xu, Kmele Foster, Batya Ungar-Sardin, Jamil Jivani, Sarah Heider, Wesley Yang, Randall Kennedy, Ralph Richard Banks, Michael Lerner, Reihan Salam, and Coleman Hughes. Racial minorities such as McWhorter, Loury, Sowell, Xu, and Helen Raleigh have said that many aspects of critical race theory are not only racist but racist against racial minorities. (McWhorter 2020) (Loury & McWhorter 2021) (Loury 2021)

Illiberalism, censorship, dogmatism, and expectations of ideological conformity oppress minorities

Expectations of ideological, political, language, and religious conformity are oppressive of minority and marginalized groups. Irshad Manji says that honest diversity requires more than different races, genders and religions, but diversity of viewpoints. (Manji 2019)

What is perplexing are the people who support the suppression of freedom of speech and expression and don't see that their speech and views would be suppressed. The freedom is what protects their right, and the right of other minority and marginalized groups, to express their views. The dominant, popularly expressed opinion needs no such protection.

In her *New York Times* column "Do Progressives Have a Free Speech Problem?", Michelle Goldberg writes, "Writing in the 1990s, at a time when feminists like Catharine MacKinnon sought to curtail free speech in the name of equality, the great left-libertarian Ellen Willis described how progressive movements sow the seeds of their own destruction when they become censorious. It's impossible, Willis wrote, 'to censor the speech of the dominant without stifling debate among all social groups and reinforcing orthodoxy within left movements.' Under such conditions, a movement can neither integrate new ideas nor build support based on genuine transformations of consciousness rather than guilt or fear of ostracism." (Goldberg 2021)

Goldberg also writes, "Cowing people is not the same as converting them."

CRT's rejection of liberalism is harmful to many minorities

Members of minority groups in the United States that often harshly criticize CRT and Kendi-style antiracism are Jews, Asians, and immigrants. Many Jewish, Asian, Hispanic, and immigrant groups have thrived under American meritocracy and liberal institutions, and object to being categorized as "white adjacent" when they do well in the system. Many Jews, Asians, and immigrants have called an attack on liberalism and meritocracy an attack on them. (Jewish Institute for Liberal Values 2021) (Weiss 2020)

San Francisco School board members were recalled by a large margin in 2022 in part after they wanted to do away with meritocracy for getting into one of the elite public schools. The biggest and most vocal demographic behind the recall was Asian-Americans, in particular Chinese-Americans. At the least, this demonstrates that there is no one voice for racial, ethnic, or other minorities and that most minorities don't agree that "we must dismantle Western society and Enlightenment ideals." (Chen 2022)

Kenny Xu writes: "The problem is that CRT implicitly defines every good societal outcome as 'white.' Based on the data, this necessarily puts Asian-Americans in a 'white adjacent' box that completely ignores their unique cultures and historical struggles. Furthermore, if being rich and successful are necessarily 'white' characteristics, the implication is that other races are not, or cannot be, successful, talented, or educated. Despite pretending to care about diversity and inclusion, CRT is actually racist in the way it implicitly categorizes groups of people." (Xu 2021)

Samuel Goldman, professor of political science and executive director of the John L. Loeb Jr. Institute for Religious Freedom at George Washington University, writes, "The reduction of American history to an unbroken story of racial oppression comes at particular cost to Jews. Because we have been among the greatest beneficiaries of liberal institutions, we are unavoidably targets when those institutions abandon or reject their liberal mission. A widely despised and persecuted people who thrived in America like nowhere else, Jews do not fit into the sharp distinction between oppressor and oppressed that characterizes ideological 'antiracism.' Therefore, Jewish experiences must either be ignored or reduced to a monolithic conception of white supremacy." (Goldman 2021)

Most Americans including minorities support meritocracy, equality, and the hope for a colorblind society

As they feel they uphold the dominant culture and oppression, fundamentalist CRT advocates and folks such as Kendi and DiAngelo are against meritocracy and the hope for a colorblind society. This view is out of step with most Americans.

Meritocracy was introduced as a revolutionary way to overcome nepotism and has been used to base occupational and educational mobility on skill. The 2020 Affirmative Action Referendum in California showed that support for meritocracy and equality had grown there, including amongst racial and ethnic minorities. (Friedersdorf)

Author Adrian Woodridge writes, "The meritocratic idea is so fundamental to modern societies that we take it for granted. We expect to be given a fair chance when we apply for a job. And we are outraged at the mere smell of nepotism or favoritism or discrimination." (Woodridge 2021)

Traditional Martin Luther King-style civil rights was premised on meritocracy and the hope for a colorblind society. Martin Luther King Jr. said, "I have a dream that my four little children will one day live in a nation where they will not be judged by the color of their skin, but by the content of their character."

Social justice activist and organizer of the March on Washington and the Southern Christian Leadership Conference Bayard Rustin famously said, "If we desire a society of peace, then we cannot achieve such a society through violence. If we desire a society without discrimination, then we must not discriminate against anyone in the process of building this society. If we desire a society that is democratic, then democracy must become a means as well as an end."

Social justice activist and congressman John R. Lewis wrote: "I've always believed that the only way we will move beyond the barriers of race is to stop seeing everything through that filter. We have to be fair, consistent, and accountable to standards higher and more universal than what particular race, age, gender, community, culture, or country each of us belongs to. There are standards of honesty, decency, and humanity that arch above all the differences that keep us apart. To appeal to those differences only continues to polarize us."

Glenn Loury writes: "Martin Luther King had the right idea with colorblindness, yet today it's regarded as a microaggression to say one doesn't see color. Of course, it's impossible literally not to see color, but despite pressure from cultural elites, we needn't give it the overarching significance we now do. In fact, if we're going to make our experiment in democracy work, we mustn't give it such significance." (Loury 2021)

Chinese immigrant Wenyan Wu writes, "Constitutional colorblindness, attacked and vilified today more than ever as a regressive tool of sociopolitical control by 'white men in power,' is the cement necessary for holding together our naturally diverse and pluralistic society. This is not to argue for indifference to divergent individual and group characteristics, but to recognize a common destiny that binds us all and overshadows our tribal differences. In the domain of public reason, colorblindness translates into an unapologetic adherence to the vision of equality, a fundamentally liberal idea rooted in equal treatment and equal access on an individual basis." (Wu 2022)

Educator Z. K. Paschal, Kenny Xu, Loury, and McWhorter see the lowering of standards to accommodate minorities as condescending and "an implicit statement of our lack of confidence in our capacity to do what others have done." Loury calls it "the bigotry of low expectations." While he believes in accommodations and some affirmative action, Loury also believes that removing meritocracy would damage universities and government. (Loury 2019) (Loury & McWhorter 2021) (Creswell 2022) (Paschal 2021) (Xu 2021)

References

al-Gharbi, M. (2020), "'Diversity Training' Doesn't Work. This Might," https://heterodoxacademy.org/blog/diversity-training-doesnt-work-this-might/

Arzoumanian, A. (2020), "Armenians and Race: A Personal Response to an Impossible Question," http://thecolgatemaroonnews.com/23987/commentary/armenians-and-race-a-personal-response-to-an-impossible-question/

Badenoch K (2020), "Full Speech on Critical Race Theory." https://www.youtube.com/watch?v=vOxdLTrS4AE

Bejan, R. (2020), "Robin DiAngelo's 'White Fragility' ignores the differences within whiteness," https://www.dal.ca/news/2020/09/01/robin-diangelo-s--white-fragility--ignores-the-differences-withi.html

Bernstein, D. (2020), "Has America Stopped Debating?", https://jewishjournal.com/cover_story/342887/has-america-stopped-debating/

Bernstein, D. (2016), "The Holocaust as 'white on white crime' and other signs of intellectual decay," https://www.washingtonpost.com/news/volokh-conspiracy/wp/2016/02/05/the-holocaust-as-white-on-white-crime-and-other-signs-of-intellectual-decay/

Bernstein, D. (2022), "In Search of Systemic Racism," https://freeblackthought.substack.com/p/in-search-of-systemic-racism

Bregman, P. (2012), "Diversity Training Doesn't Work," https://hbr.org/2012/03/diversity-training-doesnt-work?

Campbell & Manning (2018), *The Rise of Victimhood Culture*, Palgrave Macmillan

Chait, J. (2020), "Is the Anti-Racism Training Industry Just Peddling White Supremacy?", https://nymag.com/intelligencer/2020/07/antiracism-training-white-fragility-robin-diangelo-ibram-kendi.html

Chen, S. (2022), "Asian Americans flex their voting power in SF school board recall," https://www.axios.com/san-francisco-recall-school-asian-americans-edfa51e2-4127-4500-b5c6-3530942a5c6c.html

Christiansen, K. (2020), "Asset-Based Anti-Racism vs. Guilt-Based Anti-Racism: What works and what doesn't?", https://assetbasedantiracism.com

Church, J. (2019), "Robin DiAngelo's White Fragility Falls Prey to Logical Fallacies," https://merionwest.com/2019/10/16/robin-diangelos-white-fragility-theory-falls-prey-to-a-logical-fallacy/

Church, J. (2020), "Ibram Kendi's Thesis Could Use a Lot More Rigor," https://merionwest.com/2020/11/07/ibram-kendis-thesis-could-use-a-lot-more-rigor/

Cieslewicz, D. (2022), "Why I Reject Critical Race Theory: I'm a Democrat and a liberal but I find the theory unconvincing and offensive," https://urbanmilwaukee.com/2022/01/05/op-ed-why-i-reject-critical-race-theory/

Cillizza, C. (2021), "Why 'wokeness' is the biggest threat to Democrats in the 2022 election," https://www.cnn.com/2021/07/12/politics/woke-green-new-deal-defund-the-police/index.html

Citizenpath (2020), "5 Countries with the Most Immigrants," https://citizenpath.com/countries-with-the-most-immigrants/

Connor, P. (2021), "Calling Asians 'White Adjacent' Is Racist And Insulting," https://www.theamericanconservative.com/articles/calling-asians-white-adjacent-is-racist-and-insulting/

Coyne, J. (2020), "Critical Theory and Its Jewish Dilemma," https://whyevolutionistrue.com/2020/12/17/james-lindsay-on-critical-theory-and-its-jewish-problem/

Coyne, J. (2020), "The Smithsonian Institution Purveys Critical Race Theory," https://whyevolutionistrue.com/2020/07/16/the-smithsonian-institution-purveys-critical-race-theory/

Coyne, J. (2020), "'Progressophobia' demolished by Bill Maher: 'Kids, there actually was a world before you got here,'" https://whyevolutionistrue.com/2021/06/12/progressophobia-demolished-by-bill-maher-kids-there-actually-was-a-world-before-you-got-here/

Coyne, J. (2020), "What is CRT," https://whyevolutionistrue.com/2021/06/08/what-is-crt-how-to-find-out/

Coyne, J. (2022), "The On Being Project Is Located on Dakota Land," https://whyevolutionistrue.com/2022/05/22/the-on-being-project-is-located-on-dakota-land/

Creswell, M. (2022), "Closing the Racial Academic Achievement Gap: Whose Responsibility Is It?", https://freeblackthought.substack.com/p/closing-the-racial-academic-achievement?

Dobbin, and Kalev, "Why Diversity Programs Fail: And What Works Better," https://hbr.org/2016/07/why-diversity-programs-fail

Dunbar-Ortiz, R. (2020), "This is no 'nation of immigrants': Let us mourn, not celebrate, the 400-year anniversary of the Mayflower's arrival in 1620," https://www.uuworld.org/articles/no-nation-immigrants

Dunst, C. (2018), "Is antisemitism a form of racism?", www.jpost.com/Diaspora/Antisemitism/Is-antisemistism-a-form-of-racism-564712

Economic Times (2021), "Indians in US wealthier with average household earning of $123,700: Report," https://economictimes.indiatimes.com/nri/migrate/indians-in-us-wealthier-with-average-household-earning-of-123700-report/articleshow/85623601.cms?

Edmond, C. (2017), "These are the countries migrants most want to move to," https://www.weforum.org/agenda/2017/11/these-are-the-countries-migrants-want-to-move-to/

Friedersdorf, F. (2020), "Why California Rejected Racial Preferences, Again," https://www.theatlantic.com/ideas/archive/2020/11/why-california-rejected-affirmative-action-again/617049/

Gaman, M. (2021), "What History Professors Really Think About the 1619 Project," https://www.forbes.com/sites/marybethgasman/2021/06/03/what-history-professors-really-think-about-the-1619-project/?sh=651b61097a15

Goldberg, M. (2021), "Do Progressives Have a Free Speech Problem?", https://www.nytimes.com/2020/07/17/opinion/sunday/harpers-letter-free-speech.html

Goldhill, H. (2018), "The left is also guilty of unscientific dogma," https://qz.com/1177154/political-scientific-biases-the-left-is-guilty-of-unscientific-dogma-too/

Goldman, S. (2021), "What We Lose When We Lose Thomas Jefferson," https://bariweiss.substack.com/p/what-we-lose-when-we-lose-thomas?s=r

Heritage Foundation (2020), "How to Identify Critical Race Theory," https://www.heritage.org/civil-society/heritage-explains/how-identify-critical-race-theory

Hughes, C (2019), "How to Be an Anti-Intellectual: A lauded book about antiracism is wrong on its facts and in its assumptions," https://www.city-journal.org/how-to-be-an-antiracist

Hughes, C. (2020), "My Open Letter to Ibram X. Kendi," https://youtu.be/kMAYJUMpStY

Illing, S. (2019), "The post-truth prophets: Postmodernism predicted our post-truth hellscape. Everyone still hates it," https://www.vox.com/features/2019/11/11/18273141/postmodernism-donald-trump-lyotard-baudrillard

Jilani, Wilcox, and Wang (2021), "Is the American Dream dead? Not for Indian Americans," https://www.deseret.com/opinion/2021/12/16/22838432/is-the-american-dream-dead-not-for-indian-americans-parag-agrawal-sundar-pichai-marriage-tech

JILV (2020), "New Paradigms in Black-Jewish Relations," https://www.youtube.com/watch?v=FoMxV0Szb7M

JILV (2021), "Critical Social Justice Ideology and Antisemitism," https://jilv.org/wp-content/uploads/2021/09/CSJ_AntisemitismWhitePaperRv2.pdf

JILV (2021), "Letter to fellow Jews on equality and liberal values," https://jilv.org/be-heard/

Jivani, J. (2022), "Progressive Stereotypes Hurt Black Communities: Black Thought Has Always Been Inconveniently Free," https://freeblackthought.substack.com/p/progressive-stereotypes-hurt-black?utm_source=url&s=

Joseph, B. (2018), "Why Nigerian Immigrants Are One of the Most Successful Ethnic Groups in the U.S.," https://medium.com/@joecarleton/why-nigerian-immigrants-are-the-most-successful-ethnic-group-in-the-u-s-23a7ea5a0832

Kahlenberg, R. (2010), "Affirmative action should be based on class, not race," https://www.economist.com/open-future/2018/09/04/affirmative-action-should-be-based-on-class-not-race

Keller, A. (2020), "Critical Race Theory Is a Victimization Cult," http://newdiscourses.com/2020/06/critical-race-theory-victimization-cult/

Kendi, I. (2019), "Pass an Anti-Racist Constitutional Amendment," https://www.politico.com/interactives/2019/how-to-fix-politics-in-america/inequality/pass-an-anti-racist-constitutional-amendment/

Katiti, K. (2021), "We Love 'Lived Experience'... Until It Undermines the Narrative: Critical Social Justice Ideology Cannot Define Me," https://freeblackthought.substack.com/p/we-love-lived-experienceuntil-it?s=r

Knight-Laurie, R. (2021), Mason, S. (2021), "Theory of Racelessness: A Case for Antirace(ism): To Eliminate Racism We Must Eliminate

Race," https://www.newsweek.com/true-anti-racism-means-being-anti-race-opinion-1653635

Knight-Laurie, R. (2022), "Turning the Page on Wokeness," https://freeblackthought.substack.com/p/turning-the-page-on-wokeness?

Lerner, M. (1993), "Jews Are Not White," https://www.villagevoice.com/2019/07/25/the-white-issue-jews-are-not-white/

Lind, M. (2020), "Progressives are a minority in America. To win, they need to compromise," https://www.theguardian.com/us-news/commentisfree/2020/dec/19/progressives-us-democrats-power-new-deal

Lindsay, J. (2020), "No, the Woke Won't Debate You. Here's Why," https://newdiscourses.com/2020/07/woke-wont-debate-you-heres-why/

Loury, G. & McWhorter, J. (2021), "The soft bigotry of low expectations," https://www.youtube.com/watch?v=xZBb2wR3t9Q

Loury, G. (2019), "Identity Politics vs. Excellence," https://glennloury.substack.com/p/identity-politics-vs-excellence/comments?s=r

Loury, G. (2021), "Why I Don't Capitalize 'Black,'" https://www.youtube.com/watch?v=v2t6fWcc4a4

Loury, G. (2021), "Wrestle not against flesh and blood," https://freeblackthought.substack.com/p/wrestle-not-against-flesh-and-blood

Loury, G. (2022), "The Unified Field Theory of Non-Whiteness with John McWhorter," https://glennloury.substack.com/p/the-unified-field-theory-of-non-whiteness?

Lozada, C. (2020), "White fragility is real, white fragility is flawed," https://www.washingtonpost.com/outlook/2020/06/18/white-fragility-is-real-white-fragility-is-flawed/

Maher, B. (2021), "New Rule: Progressophobia; Real Time with Bill Maher (HBO)," https://www.youtube.com/watch?v=fB9KVYAdYwg

Manhattan Institute (2021), "Critical Race Theory: On the New Ideology of Race," https://www.youtube.com/watch?v=ZuvhrXM3v7U&t=4495s

Manhattan Institute (2021), "Anti-Racism and Anti-Semitism Collide: Glenn Loury in Conversation with Bari Weiss," https://www.youtube.com/watch?v=Zu9PdD9W-W8

Manji, I. (2019), "Diversity based on labels is not diversity at all," https://www.nbcnews.com/think/video/irshad-manji-diversity-based-on-labels-is-not-diversity-at-all-1452955203717

Martin, B. (2022), "Stop Voting out of Misplaced Loyalty: Vote according to your real interests, regardless of party or skin color," https://freeblackthought.substack.com/p/stop-voting-out-of-misplaced-loyalty?s=r

Mason, S. (2021), "Theory of Racelessness: A Case for Antirace(ism) To Eliminate Racism We Must Eliminate Race," https://freeblackthought.substack.com/p/theory-of-racelessness-a-case-for?s=r

McClone, P. (2020), "African American Museum site removes 'whiteness' chart," https://www.washingtonpost.com/entertainment/museums/african-american-museum-site-removes-whiteness-chart-after-criticism-from-trump-jr-and-conservative-media/2020/07/17/4ef6e6f2-c831-11ea-8ffe-372be8d82298_story.html

McWhorter & Loury (2021), "Should We Abolish Racial Categories?", https://www.youtube.com/watch?v=CCuThc89-GA

McWhorter, J. (2019), "The Origins of the 'Acting White' Charge," https://www.theatlantic.com/ideas/archive/2019/07/acting-white-charge-origins/594130/

McWhorter, J. (2020), "Linguist John McWhorter Says *White Fragility* Is Condescending Toward Black People," https://www.npr.org/2020/07/20/892943728/professor-criticizes-book-white-fragility-as-dehumanizing-to-black-people

McWhorter, J. (2020), "Why won't the woke vanguard debate?", https://www.youtube.com/watch?v=68nimcszjT4

McWhorter, J. (2021), "John McWhorter on Real Time," https://www.youtube.com/watch?v=-tjgXQDyqno

Moss, K. (2003) *The Color of Class: Poor Whites and the Paradox of Privilege*, https://www.upenn.edu/pennpress/book/13914.html

Northwest Asian Weekly (2020), "WA school district apologizes for excluding Asians as POC," https://nwasianweekly.com/2020/11/wa-school-district-apologizes-for-excluding-asians-as-poc/

Pachal, Z. (2021), "Not Some Poor Little Black Fellow," https://freeblackthought.substack.com/p/not-some-poor-little-black-fellow?s=r

Paresky, P. (2021), "Critical Race Theory and the 'Hyper-White' Jew," https://sapirjournal.org/social-justice/2021/05/critical-race-theory-and-the-hyper-white-jew/

Perry, J. (2017), "Thomas Sowell on Slavery and This Fact—There Are More Slaves Today Than Were Seized from Africa in Four Centuries," https://www.aei.org/carpe-diem/thomas-sowell-on-slavery-and-this-fact-there-are-more-slaves-today-than-were-seized-from-africa-in-four-centuries/

Pew (2012), "The Rise of Asian Americans," https://www.pewresearch.org/social-trends/2012/06/19/the-rise-of-asian-americans/

Pinker, S. (2018), "Progressophobia: Why Things Are Better Than You Think They Are," https://skepticalinquirer.org/2018/05/progressophobia-why-things-are-better-than-you-think-they-are/

Pluckrose, H. (2020), "White Fragility Training and Freedom of Belief," https://areomagazine.com/2020/06/26/is-white-fragility-training-ethical/

Pluckrose, H. (2021), "We Need Liberal Social Justice, Not 'Critical Social Justice,'" https://symposium.substack.com/p/we-need-liberal-social-justice-not?utm_source=url

Redstone, L. (2018), "A Straightforward Primer on Critical Race Theory (and Why It Matters)," https://www.forbes.com/sites/ilanaredstone/2021/07/18/a-straightforward-primer-on-critical-race-theory-and-why-it-matters/?sh=79f6e1e43212

Reuters (2007), "Chronology: Who banned slavery when?", https://www.reuters.com/article/uk-slavery/chronology-who-banned-slavery-when-idUSL15614649200703222

Rubin, J. (2020), "What Divides Us Is Class, Not Race," https://quillette.com/2020/10/24/what-divides-us-is-class-not-race/

Schlott, R. (2020), "How a 28-year-old is fighting against 'divisive' anti-racism training," https://nypost.com/2022/01/22/how-a-28-year-old-is-fighting-divisive-antiracism-training/

Schneider, A. (2019), *A Self-Proclaimed White Supremacy Culture*

Schneider, A. (2019), "Is the 'White Supremacy Culture' Paradigm a Useful Strategy for Anti-Racist/Anti-Oppression Social Justice Work?", https://drive.google.com/file/d/1Ibp-h6bLYllUSjV7qcNg9hPLA8EDoY96/view

Seager, P. (2018), "The Nine Cognitive Distortions Taught in College," https://tpseager.medium.com/the-9-cognitive-distortions-taught-in-college-d1cfa81053ea

Serwer, A. (2022), "Whoopi Goldberg's American Idea of Race," https://www.theatlantic.com/ideas/archive/2022/02/whoopi-goldbergs-american-idea-race/621470/

Shermer, M. (2013), "The Liberals' War on Science," https://www.scientificamerican.com/article/the-liberals-war-on-science/

Smith, E. (2021), "Black thought varies as widely as black individuals," https://www.freeblackthought.com

Snyder, J. (2021), "Why Ibram Kendi's Antiracism is So Flawed," https://heterodoxacademy.org/blog/why-ibram-kendis-antiracism-is-so-flawed/

Soh, G. (2017), "Are gender feminists and transgender activists undermining science?", https://www.latimes.com/opinion/op-ed/la-oe-soh-trans-feminism-anti-science-20170210-story.html

Sowell, T. (2005), "Crippled by Their Culture," https://www.wsj.com/articles/SB111448311657516833

Sowell, T. (2006), "Poisoning present by distorting slavery's past," https://www.dallasnews.com/opinion/commentary/2010/05/01/thomas-sowell-poisoning-present-by-distorting-slavery-s-past/

Sowell, T. (2010), "Facts About Slavery They Don't Teach You at School," https://www.youtube.com/watch?v=3_3wyRaCD34

Thandeka (2007), "Why Anti-Racism Will Fail," https://files.meadville.edu/files/resources/thandeka-why-anti-racism-will-fail-447.pdf

Tucker, C. (2021), "Democracy needs critical thinking," timesunion.com/opinion/article/Cynthia-Tucker-Democracy-needs-critical-thinking-16603965.php

Wooldridge, A. (2021), "The War on Meritocracy. Meritocracy made the modern world. Now the revolt against merit threatens to unmake it," https://www.persuasion.community/p/the-war-on-meritocracy?s=r

WorldAtlas (2020) "Slavery Today: Countries with the Highest Prevalence of Modern Slaves," https://www.worldatlas.com/articles/countries-with-the-most-modern-slaves-today.html

Wu, W. (2022), "On Being American," https://freeblackthought.substack.com/p/being-american

Xu, K. (2021), "Critical Race Theory Has No Idea What to Do with Asian Americans," https://www.newsweek.com/critical-race-theory-has-no-idea-what-do-asian-americans-opinion-1608984

Yglesias, M. (2021), "Tema Okun's 'White Supremacy Culture' work is bad: Prestigious universities and worthy nonprofits shouldn't push nonsense," https://www.slowboring.com/p/tema-okun?utm_source=url&s=r

Zucher, A. (2021), "Critical race theory: the concept dividing the US," https://www.bbc.com/news/world-us-canada-57908808

8 Is CRT Itself Illiberal, or Is CRT Just Sometimes Applied Illiberally?

A regular question of debate is whether critical race theory itself is dogmatic, illiberal, and authoritarian, or is it that some people use it in a dogmatic, illiberal, and authoritarian manner?

Numerous academics say that CRT is dogmatic and Orwellian. After all, CRT talks about undermining the Western Enlightenment and liberal ideas and dismantling current society. Many of Kendi's and DiAngelo's ideas are authoritarian and overtly promote the suppression of freedom of speech.

However, there are CRT advocates who are not dogmatic or illiberal. There are advocates who know that CRT is imperfect and cannot be the only lens through which to view society. They do not shame or silence people based on their race. They support due process and freedom of expression and they disagree with the divisive teaching approach of DiAngelo. While knowing more must be done and the country must do better, they agree that there has been progress in racial justice over years, along with improved rights for women, the disabled, and other minorities.

I debate CRT with a far left professor friend who calls herself "woke" and supports CRT. She does not interpret CRT in any sort of authoritarian, racially essentialist way, and considers me as an individual and not a category. She sees the dogmatists and illiberals as bad apples. She disagreed with the recent canceling of Dorian Abbott, a University of Chicago professor who had a major lecture canceled because he said he supported meritocracy. She knows that there are other forms of bigotry outside of CRT's scope. As a professor of medicine and a physician, she strongly supports science, logic, debate, and critical thinking.

Constitutional and education law professor Evan Gerstman writes that the backlash against CRT isn't against the theory itself but against the methods some use to teach it, such as singling out and shaming students. He writes, "The best way to address the backlash to CRT would be to recognize that, despite good intentions, there are abuses done in its name. What most critics of CRT want is for those abuses to stop. Unfortunately, many progressives have mimicked the tactics of the most paleo-conservative defenders of the police. They deny there are any abuses, and, when confronted with incontrovertible evidence of abuse, they write it off as the work of a few bad apples." (Gerstman 2021)

University of Chicago's Jerry Coyne writes that there are different versions and interpretations of CRT. This means that one should judge people or groups by what they do and specifically say, as opposed to merely by whether or not they support CRT.

Coyne suggests that, as it means and suggests so many things to different people, the term critical race theory should be dropped from our vocabulary.

Many within the Left and the Right misunderstand and distort what CRT is

Coyne and sociology professor Ilana Redstone write that people both within the political right and left mischaracterize CRT for their political purposes. (Redstone 2018)

Coyne says the left media and politicians tend to whitewash CRT and its use, such as deceptively saying, "It's only a legal theory used in law schools and is not taught in elementary schools," and falsely saying, "It's merely the real, objective history of race and slavery in the United States." Coyne says that, on the other hand, the right media and politicians tend to overstate CRT and use it to prevent much racial justice education and minimize the effects of racism. (Coyne 2022)

Coyne writes, "a pox on both ideological houses." However, he says that, between the two, the political right's description of CRT tends to be more accurate. (Coyne 2021)

My experience is that most people in both the left and right who post idle opinions or memes about it on Facebook or Twitter have badly distorted ideas of what it is. They get their distorted and often outright false conceptions of it from their preferred partisan news sources.

There is pushback against CRT and "woke culture" from within both the right and the left

A common false talking point within the left and left media is characterizing all who criticize critical race theory and "woke culture" as alt-right, right-wing, and Republican. (Yang 2022)

There has been much pushback and criticism from within the left and Democratic and Socialist parties and even commonly from economic Marxists. Numerous left academics have criticized critical race theory and woke culture, including John McWhorter, Steven Pinker, Irshad Manji, Jonathan Haidt, and Coyne. Most of those whom I personally know who oppose CRT and woke culture are on the left, and include Social Democrats.

Former Madison Wisconsin Mayor Dave Cieslewicz wrote, "I am a liberal and a Democrat but I find the theory unconvincing and offensive." Seattle Socialist City Council member Kshama Sawant, who is about as far left as one can find in American politics, is against "woke Democrats and cancel culture" because she feels it works against multiracial working-class unity. Former Bill Clinton campaign manager James Carville famously criticized "stupid wokeness" and "faculty lounge" language such as Latinx "that no one else uses" for costing the Democratic Party elections. (Cieslewicz 2022) (Hedges 2022) (Illing 2021) (Trudo & Parnes 2021)

References

Coyne, J. (2022), "Why both Left and Right distort CRT for political ends," https://whyevolutionistrue.com/2022/01/28/why-both-left-and-right-distort-crt-for-political-ends/

Cieslewicz, D. (2022), "Why I Reject Critical Race Theory," https://urbanmilwaukee.com/2022/01/05/op-ed-why-i-reject-critical-race-theory/

Illing, S. (2021), "James Carville on the state of Democratic politics," https://www.vox.com/22338417/james-carville-democratic-party-biden-100-days

Trudo and Parnes (2021), "'Woke' discussion simmers for Democrats," https://thehill.com/homenews/administration/581196-woke-discussion-simmers-for-democrats/

Gerstman, E. (2021), "Denying the Abuses of Critical Race Theory and Cancel Culture," https://www.forbes.com/sites/evangerstmann/2021/08/02/denying-the-abuses-of-critical-race-theory-and-cancel-culture/?sh=6260b0be18d3

Redstone, L. (2018), "A Straightforward Primer on Critical Race Theory (and Why It Matters)," https://www.forbes.com/sites/ilanaredstone/2021/07/18/a-straightforward-primer-on-critical-race-theory-and-why-it-matters/?sh=79f6e1e43212

Yang W (2022), "Yes, Things Are Really As Bad As You've Heard", https://wesleyyang.substack.com/p/yes-things-are-really-as-bad-as-youve?

9 These All Are Topics for Discussion and Debate

Critical race theory, racism, and social and institutional organization are exceedingly complex topics. Even amongst critical race theorists there is a diversity of interpretations and approaches. DiAngelo and Kendi disagree with each other in areas.

The previous three chapters have presented a wide variety of views and insights, any of which is up for fair debate. Most people will mix and match ideas from the previous chapters, and incorporate other theories, models, and ideologies. While I have my view, I don't pretend to have the final, objective answer. No one has the final, objective answer.

These topics in the public and private arenas too often involve heated debates full of ad hominem attacks, emotional reasoning, and people talking past each other. The goal of this book is to support conversation with sincere listening and consideration of different views.

10 Extreme Social Justice Activism as a Religion

Numerous academics and experts have compared the dogmatic use of critical race theory and the Unitarian Universalist Association's extreme, authoritarian version of antiracism ideology to a fundamentalist Evangelical religion. Writes political scientist Art Keller, "It is not a particularly unique observation to notice that the Critical Social Justice movement, particularly the part that embraces Critical Race Theory, bears tremendous resemblance to a secular religion." (Keller 2020)

The ideology is full of Abrahamic ideas of original sin, spiritual awakening ("woke"), blasphemy, thought and expression control, suspension of disbelief, believers versus unbelievers, moral versus immoral, repentance, admission of sin, submission to authority, binary thinking, and calling those who do not fully subscribe to the theory immoral ("racists," "upholders of white supremacy"). The Unitarian Universalist Association's *UU World* magazine and UU leaders regularly describe it in religious terms and imagery, calling their work "liberation theology."

Former Unitarian Universalist Sasha Kwapinski wrote, "The comparison with religious fundamentalism is spot on. I turned away from fundamentalist Christianity decades ago largely due to their hammering about how we are (supposedly) collectively guilty or culpable due to Adam's transgression in the Garden of Eden. Collective 'white guilt' is little more than an updated, politically correct remake of the same fictional concept."

Sociology professors Bradley Campbell, of California State University Los Angeles, and Jason Manning, of the University of West Virginia, write: "I think it's similar to a lot of utopian political movements in having similarities to religion. Those at the forefront of the movement, who wholeheartedly embrace an oppression/victimhood worldview derived from Critical Theory, and who see it as providing a basis for a call for repentance and change in their own lives and the lives of others, and as a call to restructure social institutions, seem to have embraced something very much like a religion." (Campbell & Manning 2018)

John McWhorter is the author of the book *Woke Racism: How a New Religion Has Betrayed Black America.* He explains not only how he believes the form of antiracism derived from current critical race theory is a religion, but how it hurts racial justice.

McWhorter says, "Anti-racism, as currently configured, has gone a long way from what used to be considered intelligent and sincere civil rights activism. Today it is a religion. And I don't mean that as a rhetorical feint. It is what any naïve anthropologist would recognize as a religion." (McWhorter 2019)

Author and Unitarian Universalist Jim Aikin writes, "McWhorter's thesis is that the adherents of 'woke' antiracism are practicing a new religion. It's not just similar to a religion; it *is* a religion. There's no higher power, but all of the other components are there. There are celebrity preachers, deadly sins, heretics (who are, inevitably, in need of persecution), a complete rejection of logic, and much more. The woke anti-racist crowd are as fully committed to their faith as Pentecostals or Scientologists." (Aikin 2022)

In his landmark 1953 social psychology book *The True Believer: Thoughts on the Nature of Mass Movements,* Eric Hoffer wrote how fanatical social, political, and religious movements tell their followers to reject logic and reason and chastise and shame dissenters or even those who merely ask questions. Notice this with fundamentalist promoters of the new social justice ideology. Hoffer wrote how the movements do not see people as individuals but as categories. Again, a hallmark of dogmatic CRT.

Wrote Hoffer, "Mass movements aggressively promote the use of doctrines that elevate faith over reason and serve as fact-proof screens between the faithful and the realities of the world. The doctrine of the mass movement must not be questioned under any circumstances."

McWhorter says there is no point in trying to debate the social justice true believers as they consider their views dogma. Critical race theory critic James Lindsay writes, "Debate and conversation, especially when they rely upon reason, rationality, science, evidence, epistemic adequacy, and other Enlightenment-based tools of persuasion, are the very thing they think produced injustice in the world in the first place. Those are not their methods and they reject them." (Lindsay 2020)

Jerry Coyne and philosopher Peter Boghossian point out that critical race theory dogmatists consider questioning of and debates about their hardcore beliefs to be taboo and "harmful." Coyne writes, "What's clear is that the Socratic Method won't work on 'woke' students, since they're unwilling to question or even defend their ideology." (Coyne 2022)

Fundamentalism and dogmatism are a psychology, and fundamentalists and zealots are a psychological type. An Emory

University study showed that far-left authoritarians share key personality traits with the far-right. (Clark 2021)

Wrote Hoffer: "Though they seem to be at opposite poles, fanatics of all kinds are actually crowded together at one end. It is the fanatic and the moderate who are poles apart and never meet. The fanatics of various hues eye each other with suspicion and are ready to fly at each other's throat. But they are neighbors and almost of one family. They hate each other with the hatred of brothers."

Psychologist Valery Tarico was raised an Evangelical Christian and studies evangelical movements. She writes that the current fundamentalist far-left social justice movements informed by critical race theory remarkably resemble the fundamentalist evangelical Christianity she left.

In the essay "The Righteous and the Woke—Why Evangelicals and Social Justice Warriors Trigger Me in the Same Way," Tarico writes, "It occurred to me recently that my time in Evangelicalism and subsequent journey out have a lot to do with why I find myself reactive to the spread of Woke culture among colleagues, political soulmates, and friends. Christianity takes many forms, with Evangelicalism being one of the more single-minded, dogmatic, groupish, and enthusiastic among them. The Woke—meaning progressives who have 'awoken' to the idea that oppression is the key concept explaining the structure of society, the flow of history, and virtually all of humanity's woes—share these qualities. To a former Evangelical, something feels too familiar—or better said, a bunch of somethings feel too familiar." (Tarico 2019)

Critical race theory is a political ideology. However, anything, including a political ideology, can be taken so fanatically while invoking higher ideals that it can become a quasi-religion. The UUA has done exactly that, couching it in theological rhetoric and religious ideas. Besides, Hoffer observes, whether they are political, social, or religious, fanatical movements are in many aspects interchangeable.

Recommended further reading:

Book: *Woke Racism: How a New Religion Has Betrayed Black America* by John McWhorter

Book: *The True Believer: Thoughts on the Nature of Mass Movements* by Eric Hoffer

References

Aikin, J. (2022), "McWhorter's Book on Woke Anti-Racism," https://midiguru.wordpress.com/2022/01/25/woke-joke/

Coyne, J. (2022), "Why both Left and Right distort CRT for political ends," https://whyevolutionistrue.com/2022/01/28/why-both-left-and-right-distort-crt-for-political-ends/

Coyne, J. (2022), "Peter Boghossian confronts Portland State students on the issue of gender," https://whyevolutionistrue.com/2022/05/29/peter-boghossian-confronts-portland-state-students-on-the-issue-of-gender/

Campbell & Manning (2018), *The Rise of Victimhood Culture*, Palgrave Macmillan

Clark, C. (2021), "Left-wing authoritarians share key psychological traits with far right, Emory study finds," https://news.emory.edu/stories/2021/09/esc_left_wing_authoritarians_psychology/campus.html?

Keller, A. (2020), "Critical Race Theory Is a Victimization Cult," http://www.newdiscourses.com/2020/06/critical-race-theory-victimization-cult

Lindsay, J. (2020), "No, the Woke Won't Debate You. Here's Why," https://newdiscourses.com/2020/07/woke-wont-debate-you-heres-why/

McWhorter, J. (2019), "How Anti Racism Hurts Black People," https://www.youtube.com/watch?v=mT2rlJe9cuU

Tarico, V. (2019), "The Righteous and the Woke—Why Evangelicals and Social Justice Warriors Trigger Me in the Same Way," https://valerietarico.com/2019/01/24/the-righteousness-and-the-woke-why-evangelicals-and-social-justice-warriors-trigger-me-in-the-same-way

11 Language as an Ideological Tool

Authoritarian political, social, and religious movements use language to try to force ideological and political conformity.

All areas have jargon, from religion to science to baseball. Jargon has a functional purpose. However, it is sometimes associated with groupthink, conformity, and cliques.

CRT and CRT-influenced antiracism acolytes and the new UUA have their ideological language: White supremacy and white supremacy culture, whiteness, dismantle, centering and decentering, BIPOC, accountable, complicit, microaggressions, colonize, intersectionality, erase/erased, etc.

Psychologist Valerie Tarico writes that the woke insider jargon is very similar in nature and purpose to the insider jargon of Christian Evangelicals:

> "Like many other groups, the saved and the Woke signal insider status by using special language. An Evangelical immediately recognizes a fellow tribe-member when he or she hears phrases like *Praise the Lord, born again, backsliding, stumbling block, give a testimony, a harvest of souls,* or *It's not a religion; it's a relationship.* The Woke signal their wokeness with words like *intersectionality, cultural appropriation, trigger warning, microaggression, privilege, fragility, problematic,* or *decolonization.* The language of the Woke may have more meaningful real-world referents than that of Evangelicals, but in both cases, jargon isn't merely a tool for efficient or precise communication as it is in many professions—it is a sign of belonging and moral virtue." (Tarico 2019)

Multiple national polls have shown that not only are substantially large majorities of all racial and ethnic demographics against politically correct culture and the politically correct language adopted by the UUA, *UU World*, UU ministers, and many UU congregations, but the top three are American Indians (88%), Latinos (87%), and Asians (82%). Seventy-five percent of black Americans were against PC culture and language. (ThinkNow 2019) (Monk 2018) (McWhorter 2022)

Linguist and black-English expert John McWhorter wrote that the term "BIPOC" is unpopular with and seen as culturally elitist by most racial minorities. A Latino pollster found that "[w]hen it came to 'Latinx,' there was near unanimity. Despite its usage by academics and cultural influencers, 98% of Latinos prefer other terms to describe their ethnicity. Only 2% of our respondents said the label accurately describes them, making it the least popular ethnic label among Latinos." Some Latinos have called white people using Latinx "Anglo-Imperialist," "Anglicizing our language," "culturally ignorant," and "English speakers imposing their social norms on other cultures." (Thinknow 2018) (Douthat 2019) (McWhorter 2022) (Cunningham 2017)

Redefining common words

Authoritarian ideologues often take common emotionally loaded and often inflammatory words, such as racist and white supremacy, and change their definitions to support their ideology.

Writes Unitarian Universalist and author Jim Aikin: "The differences between the KKK and a UU congregation could not possibly be more stark. To use the term 'white supremacy culture' to refer to anything in UU culture is flatly preposterous. I can understand why the term is being used, however: Its shock value is undeniable. It's a verbal hand grenade. Nonetheless, it's a mistake. Using the term—flinging it freely without attempting to define what you mean by it—is going to alienate a lot of sensible people. People you would like to have on your side. People like me." (Aikin 2019)

Progressive Democrat and former Mayor of Madison Wisconsin Dave Cieslewicz writes, "It's hard to start a useful conversation with an insult. For example, up until about a year ago, 'white supremacy' was a phrase reserved for neo-Nazis. Now, we're told that we're all white supremacists. Well, no, actually I'm not. And I'll bet you're not either, but I sure don't like the sound of it and it doesn't make me more receptive to the arguments of those who think this way." (Cieslewicz 2022)

In the 2019 paper "Is the 'White Supremacy Culture' Paradigm a Useful Strategy for Anti-Racist/Anti-Oppression Social Justice Work?", political science professor Anne L. Schneider writes about "the dangers of progressive/liberal people and groups adopting illiberal strategies including the use of words like 'white supremacy' to describe liberal and progressive organizations that do not hold beliefs or practices that portray the white race as superior to other races." She believes that such language hurts racial justice work by dividing rather than unifying would-be allies in the causes. (Schneider 2019)

Arguing that racism now confusingly has too many conflicting definitions, McWhorter writes: "The key difference is between outright bigotry and the more abstract operations of what we call 'systemic racism.' Yes, there is a synergy between the two. But as the difficulty in our conversations about racism attests, there is a wide gulf between personal prejudice (Racism 1.0) and the societal and sociohistorical operations that render Black physicists, for example, rare relative to Black people's proportion of the population—Racism 2.0, sometimes even termed 'white supremacy.' In an alternate universe, those two things might not go under the same name." (McWhorter 2022)

Expanding a word to encompass everything under the sun is bad practice. It's also counterproductive as it dilutes the power and meaning of the word. When everything is "racism" and "white supremacy"—from being a member of the KKK to asking someone, "Have you been to Paris?" (Supposedly a microaggression, as it assumes they have the privilege to travel abroad) to using Robert's Rules in a meeting—the words not only lose all meaning but people will quit taking them seriously.

I've noticed that the UUA Facebook page and *UU World* magazine like to use the term "white supremacy" to make rhetorical and emotional associations of, say, the use of Robert's Rules in a UU board meeting with a KKK supporter going on a mass murder spree ("They're both 'white supremacy'"). That's where the word has too many meanings, and the UUA's association of the two comes across as intentional rhetorical sleight of hand. UUs using Robert's Rules are not on a slippery slope to or a step away from KKK lynchings or a racist mass shooting, and the UUA should quit implying that they are. That's why it's bad practice to put everything under the sun under the umbrella of one word.

One person said, "If everything is racism then nothing is racism."

Words as tools of intimidation

Accusatory and shaming language is often used to keep people in line, to intimidate and shut them up. "Racist" and "white supremacy" are inflammatory words to most, and people fear being labeled with them.

Social critic Shelby Steele writes that white people "have this vulnerability to being disarmed of moral authority by being called a racist." McWhorter writes, "America is falling under the grips of this ideology out of neither serious counsel nor consensus, but fear. For most Americans, being called a racist is all but equivalent to being called a pedophile." (Steele 2006)

Keith Swanson wrote: "The weapon of choice is to call a person a racist. If that is not strong enough, then they use the term white supremacist. Once you are branded as a racist, there is no defense. It would be reasonable to be able to actually discuss whether such and such an action is racist or not, but that is simply not possible: once branded you are tarnished."

Tarico writes: "Shaming and shunning have ancient roots as tools of social control, and they elevate the status of the person or group doing the shaming. Maoist struggle sessions (forced public confessions) and Soviet self-criticism are examples of extreme shaming in social-critical movements seeking to upend traditional power structures. So, it should be no surprise that some of the Woke show little hesitation when call-out opportunities present themselves—nor that some remain unrelentingly righteous even when those call-outs leave a life or a family in ruins." (Tarico 2019)

Soviet-born American professor Anna Krylov writes, "In Soviet times, those who opposed the Party line were called 'enemies of the people'; now they are called 'racists.'" (Krylov & Tanzman 2021)

Language as an Orwellian tool of indoctrination and thought control

I understand the need for some to have a shared group language. However, someone who communicates in this language can be using it to express an ideology. A church that speaks in these terms is speaking in an ideology. Those who expect you to use their ideological language are trying to create ideological conformity. (Soriano 2010)

In her essay "Language as an Instrument of Totalitarianism," Alexandra Kapelos-Peters writes, "In order to maintain its power, George Orwell claims, a political regime uses language to produce a reduced state of individual consciousness in its residents. As it structures and places limits on ideas that an individual is capable of forming, language is established as a type of mind-control for the masses. The primary purpose of political language is to eliminate individual thought and expression." (Kapelos-Peters 2003)

Political theorist Saul Alinksy famously said, "He who controls the language controls the masses."

While all should work to be conscious of others' linguistic sensibilities and avoid using words that are universally felt to be offensive, freedom of thought and belief requires freedom of language.

References:

Aikin, J. (2019), "Shut Up! You're Not Liberal Enough!", https://midiguru.wordpress.com/2019/06/24/shut-up-youre-not-liberal-enough/

Kapelos-Peters, A. (2003), "Language as an Instrument of Totalitarianism," https://www.alexandrakp.com/text/2003-03/language-as-an-instrument-of-totalitarianism/

Krylov A & Tanzman J (2021), "Academic Ideologues Are Corrupting STEM. The Silent Liberal Majority Must Fight Back", https://quillette.com/2021/12/18/scientists-must-gain-the-courage-to-oppose-the-politicization-of-their-disciplines

McWhorter, J. (2022), "BIPOC is Jargon. That's OK, and Normal People Don't Have to Use It," https://www.nytimes.com/2022/03/25/opinion/bipoc-latinx.html

McWhorter, J. (2022), "Racism Has Too Many Definitions. We Need Another Term," https://www.nytimes.com/2022/05/17/opinion/buffalo-racism.html

Monk, Y. (2018), "Americans Strongly Dislike PC Culture," http://theatlantic.com/ideas/archive/2018/10/large-majorities-dislike-political-correctness/572581/

Soriano, R. (2010), "Manipulation of language as a weapon of mind control and abuse of power in *1984*," https://rorueso.blogs.uv.es/2010/10/28/manipulation-of-language-as-a-weapon-of-mind-control-and-abuse-of-power-in-1984/

Schneider, A. (2019), "Is the 'White Supremacy Culture' Paradigm a Useful Strategy for Anti-Racist/Anti-Oppression Social Justice Work?", https://drive.google.com/file/d/1Ibp-h6bLYllUSjV7qcNg9hPLA8EDoY96/view

Steele, J. (2006), "White Guilt and the End of the Civil Rights Era," https://www.npr.org/templates/story/story.php?storyId=5385701

Tarico, V. (2019), "The Righteous and the Woke—Why Evangelicals and Social Justice Warriors Trigger Me in the Same Way," https://valerietarico.com/2019/01/24/the-righteousness-and-the-woke-why-evangelicals-and-social-justice-warriors-trigger-me-in-the-same-way

ThinkNow (2019), "Progressive Latino pollster: 98% of Latinos do not identify with 'Latinx' label," http://medium.com/@ThinkNowTweets/progressive-latino-pollster-trust-me-latinos-do-not-identify-with-latinx-63229adebcea

12 Intolerance and Illiberalism: How to Make Universities Mediocre

There has been much talk about illiberalism and "woke intolerance" in institutions, focusing here on universities. There is no question that censorship, illiberalism, and intolerance have long existed within the political far right. However, such qualities are now also associated with social justice and identity politics areas within the far left. New York University social psychology professor Jonathan Haidt said, "Most people are horrified at what's going on at universities." (MTC 2016)

The following are several of the more egregious recent examples of illiberalism on campuses:

Skidmore College student activists called for the firing of and boycotting the classes of art professor David Peterson because he observed a Pro Police rally. They also called for the firing of his wife even though she was not employed by the university. Peterson said he and his wife didn't go to support the rally but to watch out of curiosity. (Churchill 2020) (Soave 2020)

Local newspaper journalist Chris Churchill wrote: "A supposedly damning photo of the Petersons circulated by students shows them standing at the rally, which was advertised as a 'positive, all-inclusive event' designed to humanize and support officers. The Petersons weren't wearing pro-police T-shirts. They weren't carrying a banner, holding a sign, or waving a black-and-blue flag. They appear to just be listening. But merely listening to an opinion that some Skidmore students find objectionable is apparently enough to get a professor in hot water." (Churchill 2020)

UCLA accounting professor Gordon Klein was suspended and publicly called out by the Business School Dean because he told a student that he would not grade black students differently nor delay their tests following the George Floyd riots in Minneapolis. The university's Faculty Code of Conduct prohibits engaging in race-based discrimination, the failure to hold exams as scheduled, and to evaluate students other than their course performance. The California Constitution forbids race-based discrimination in education. Klein, who also is a lawyer, said, "I was following university policy meticulously in refusing to discriminate." (Morey 2020) (Klein 2020) (UCLA 2019)

St. Olaf College philosophy professor Edmund Santurri was the Director of the school's Institute for Freedom and Community. With a slogan of "Dialogue that opens minds," the institute's mission is to bring in prominent speakers to expose students to heterodox ideas. Santurri was removed as director after a group of students protested that they didn't like some of the views of speaker Peter Singer, a Princeton bioethics professor and one of the world's preeminent moral philosophers. (Morey 2022)

A headline read, "St. Olaf ousts faculty director of institute dedicated to bringing controversial speakers to campus—because speakers caused controversy."

University of Chicago climate scientist Dorian Abbot co-wrote with Stanford business professor Ivan Marinovic an op-ed piece arguing for meritocracy in student admissions, faculty hiring, and the bestowing of awards. This is a position held by most Americans, including minorities. Student activists petitioned for Abbot to be removed from a position, and, under pressure from a

Twitter campaign, MIT canceled a prestigious annual public science lecture he was scheduled to give. (Abbot 2021) (Small 2021) (Abbot & Marinovic)

Scholar Robert P. George wrote that the decision to cancel Abbot's lecture was "chilling to academic freedom and free speech." (Sobey 2021)

University of Southern California business school foreign languages professor Greg Patton was publicly called out by the Dean and removed from teaching for using in a lecture the Mandarin word for "that" (那个, pronounced nà ge or neige), which sounds similar to an English-language racial epithet. He had taught the class dozens of times over ten years with no complaint. (McGahan 2020) (Agrawal 2020) (Nakagome 2020)

The irony was that, as USC has a large ethnic Chinese population, there was a backlash against the university's actions. Ethnic Chinese on campus and beyond decried it as anti-Asian bigotry with the professor being punished for speaking Chinese. It made newspaper headlines in China, and Chinese graduates of the business school signed a letter likening the university's actions to Mao's Cultural Revolution. (Volokh 2020) (Stevens 2020)

Further, a survey showed how outraged and scared were many of Patton's colleagues. Quotes from different professors included:

"There was no judge, jury, or anything, only cancellation. If faculty with long records of good performance can lose reputation in a flash or parts of their job for this kind of five-second mix-up, which can happen to anybody by accident given how much material we have to cover, it means we will become a society where people always talk slow, prescreen every word, and take the safest possible route on everything they say. By nature, that will make us irrelevant."

"It makes me frightened to teach students who can have a faculty member removed for giving an innocuous example in another language. It makes me feel like the dean's office is willing to throw faculty under the bus in order [to] preserve the appearance of diversity and inclusion instead of opening up dialogues on both sides."

"I will never teach about anything having to do with diversity, or touching on anything having to do with diversity, if I can at all help it. It will clearly get me fired, regardless of how well I do it."

The question is whether these and other instances of ridiculous overreactions are aberrations, or are they representative of a general trend.

Veronique de Rugy and Tevi Troy of George Mason University's Mercatus Center and Samuel Abrams of Sarah Lawrence University see a widespread increase in campus intolerance. However, Columbia University political science professor Jeffrey Adams Sachs does not. Haidt sees a rise in illiberalism but sees it primarily in East Coast elite schools, including Ivy League schools, and in areas on the West Coast. Haidt wrote, "The academic world in the social sciences is a monoculture—except in economics, which is the only social science that has some real diversity. Anthropology and sociology are the worst—those fields seem to be really hostile and rejecting toward people who aren't devoted to social justice." (Troy 2021) (Morey 2020) (Sachs 2019) (MTG 2016)

Polls have shown that professors are increasingly politically left. However, professors' political persuasions are not an inherent problem when the professors and schools allow a diversity of views and debate. I studied at a famously progressive private university and in a humanities department with a clear political and ideological slant. The professors not only allowed but encouraged debate and the expression of a diversity of ideas in the classroom. Well argued dissent and outside-the-box thinking were rewarded. (PRI 2019)

Polls show that "intolerance is on the rise" among university students. Incoming freshmen are more willing to shut down speech they find offensive and more willing to ban extreme speakers. In turn, a survey showed that 80 percent of students self-censor out of fear of being criticized or called out. A liberal arts college professor wrote that "not a week goes by that I don't hear from frustrated students who feel they cannot speak freely." (HERI 2019) (Rampell 2016) (Harden 2021) (Abrams 2021)

Illiberalism, censorship, and intolerance are bad for students, education and research

Liberalism, freedom of speech, and the exchange of a diversity of ideas are essential for a university and for education. They are necessary for creativity and learning. Students must learn to listen to and consider different opinions and views. This is how they expand their minds and gain knowledge, how they prepare for the multicultural world. Studies have shown that students who have friends with different views become more tolerant and open-minded. (Higher Ed 2020)

Such freedom of thought and inquiry and diversity of ideological and political views are necessary for quality academic research.

Social psychologist and research fellow Sean Stevens writes about the new illiberalism: "Research and scholarship will suffer. . . . Why place one's job, or even one's career, at risk by investigating a politically controversial topic or worse, publishing a finding that reaches a conclusion that is politically unpalatable to most of your colleagues?" (Stevens 2021)

In her 2021 *Journal of Physical Chemistry Letters* paper 'The Peril of Politicizing Science,' Ukrainian-born and Russian-educated University of Southern California chemistry professor Anna Krylov wrote that she sees a similar type of ideological corruption of academic science research as in the former Soviet Union. (Krylov 2021) (Krylov & Tanzman 2021)

Haidt says that, whether it's found in political parties, areas of study, or social movements, groupthink that stifles dissent and heterodoxy is "structurally stupid" and will usually come to wrong conclusions and make foolish decisions. "Whatever they are doing, it's probably wrong." (Loury and Haidt 2022)

What are the Causes Beyond the New Illiberalism and Intolerance?

Psychologists, sociologists, political scientists, and philosophers have identified the following intertwined influences behind the new woke intolerance and illiberalism on some campuses.

Infantilization of students

Everyone should be aware of racism and other bigotry including in the dominant culture and language. We all have much to learn; we must listen and be sensitive to others' perspectives and experiences. However, sensitivity can move to the extremes of fanaticism.

Jonathan Haidt says that safe spaces, excessive focus on microaggressions, and the idea of being emotionally "harmed" by words and ideas are not only bad for campuses and education but bad for students' health. Campuses that are illiberal and intolerant are emotionally and educationally stunting young people. Haidt and education lawyer Greg Lukianoff have written extensively about this in the book *The Coddling of the American Mind: How Good Intentions and Bad Ideas Are Setting Up a Generation for Failure*. (Haidt 2018)

This is all done in the name of emotional well-being. Many students are being taught to be emotionally fragile and immature and that they must be protected from the normal tribulations of everyday life.

Haidt says that many young people have been taught that their subjective feelings are truth and that it is wrong and harmful for these feelings to be countered. Minorities' subjective opinions are treated as indisputable truth-telling, and activists say it causes "harm" to even question their truths or ask for evidence. This leads to a stifling of debate and inquiry and a lack of due process in disputes. In the earlier examples, the professors were often punished without hearings. For the administrators, subjective claims of harm from a small group of students were all that was needed.

The climate is bad not only for learning but for the students' mental health. Young people must be exposed to a diversity of ideas, views, and challenges to grow into emotionally healthy and resilient people. Teaching young people that their subjective feelings are unquestionable truths is not only false but child abuse. It leaves them unable to function and cope in the real world, where not everyone will agree with or defer to them and where they will not always be correct. It contributes to mental health problems, including anxiety, depression, and cognitive distortion. (Haidt 2018) (Haidt 2019)

Psychologist Valerie Tarico writes, "Given these dynamics, it shouldn't be surprising that some activists develop habits that can be hard on psychological and relationship health." (Tarico 2021)

It becomes so extreme that a population of students demand trigger warnings to prevent them from encountering words and ideas they don't like.

Harvard law students asked professors not to teach rape law and not even use the word "violation," as in "a violation of the law," because it might cause distress. Law students called for the firing of University of Illinois Chicago professor Jason Kilborne because he used witness court testimony on a test that included a redacted racial epithet and the redacted word 'bitch.' He intentionally used the type of testimony the future lawyers would regularly encounter in court. (Gerson 2014) (Jacobson 2021)

Harvard law professor Jeannie Suk Gerson compared this to trying to teach "a medical student who is training to be a surgeon but who fears that he'll become distressed if he sees or handles blood." (Gerson 2014)

A culture of victimhood and a new caste system

Sociology professors Bradley Campbell and Jason Manning have researched and written extensively about how there is a new victimhood culture on campuses and elsewhere. (Campbell and Manning 2018)

They have written how social justice activists have created a new caste system where those who deem themselves most "marginalized" are morally and socially superior to others. Haidt identifies the groups that are currently treated as "sacred": racial minorities, LGBTs, Latinos, Native Americans, women, people with disabilities, and Muslims. White, heterosexual males are at the bottom. An individual's place in the caste system and the value of one's opinions are not based on personal character or merit, but on such things as the color of one's skin and one's ethnicity and gender. (Friedersdorf 2020) (Campbell & Manning 2018)

Hallmarks of victimhood culture are taking offense and expressing outrage at perceived microaggressions, censorship of opposing views, trying to prevent presentations by heterodox speakers, demanding safe spaces, politically correct language, publicly calling out and shaming perceived heretics, and characterizing people with different views as immoral. (Friedersdorf 2020) (Campbell & Manning 2018)

Campbell and Manning wrote: "The combination of high sensitivity with dependence on others encourages people to emphasize or exaggerate the severity of offenses. There's a corresponding tendency to emphasize one's degree of victimization, one's vulnerability to harm, and one's need for assistance and protection. People who air grievances are likely to appeal to such concepts as disadvantage, marginality, or trauma, while casting the conflict as a matter of oppression. . . . The result is that this culture also emphasizes a particular source of moral worth: victimhood. Victim identities are deserving of special care and deference. Contrariwise, the privileged are morally suspect if not deserving of outright contempt. Privilege is to victimhood as cowardice is to honor." (Lehman 2018)

Former Yale professor William Deresiewicz writes that, unlike Vietnam War protests in the 1960s, the campus social justice crusaders are not protesting against institutional authority but appealing to it. This relates to the childlike fragility described by Haidt, with the students seeking protection. Haidt said that such appealing to authority "makes sense in situations when you're talking about children; when reaching adulthood, however, students and potential employees should be able to navigate social interactions (even unpleasant but not harassing ones) themselves." (Deresiewicz 2015) (Haidt and Lukianoff 2021)

John McWhorter and Glenn Loury say that, unlike previous civil rights movements, these students portray themselves as weak, not strong. The two professors say the claims of harm and the need for emotional protection and safe places often are transparent performances used to gain power and social status. Virtue signaling is defined as a hollow public display to raise one's social and perceived moral status over others. (Loury & McWhorter 2022)

Education scholar and lawyer George Leef writes, "Once students figured out that declaring themselves to be victims of an evil society gave them a great deal of power, a culture of victimhood rapidly spread across our college campuses." (Leef 2021)

Viewing one's identity primarily and inescapably as that of a victim is mentally unhealthy and dysfunctional, contributing to depression, anxiety, and other disorders. Teaching children a victim mentality and to view the world and people through a binary victim versus oppressor lens is a form of child abuse that sets them up for a lifetime of failure, unhappiness, and unhealthy relationships. (WebMD 2022) (Tarico 2021)

Social Justice ideologies that are illiberal and dogmatic

Extreme social justice activists not only use the victimhood caste system but present their ideologies as dogma. Even minor deviation from accepted ideas and ideological language can elicit coordinated public attack and censorship. (Demaske 2020)

Dogmatic and zealous adoption of these ideologies, such as on some university campuses, clamp down on standard educational methods of debate, free inquiry, and the exchange of ideas.

Hyperpartisanship

Compounding this, things have become hyperpartisan in much of American society. Some Americans believe that people with different views are not just wrong but bad, making it easier to silence and punish them.

A 2020 *Scientific American* report noted that many Americans have "a basic abhorrence for their opponents—an 'othering' in which a group conceives of its rivals as wholly alien in every way. This toxic form of polarization has fundamentally altered political discourse, public civility, and even the way politicians govern." In her *New York Times* column "America Has a Scorn Problem," Anglican priest Trish Warren Harrison wrote, "We find one another repugnant—not just wrong but bad. Our rhetoric casts the arguments of others as profound moral failings." (Aschwanden 2020) (Pew 2019) (Harrison 2021)

This destructive tribalism is not merely between the right and left but within both the right and the left. Within the left these days, radicals attack liberals and moderates, resulting in circular firing squads and the "left eating their own." (Harris 2022)

There are brilliant thinkers all along the political spectrum. Even though you aren't going to agree with everything they say, it's your loss to not listen to the sharp minds on both sides of the aisle.

Intelligent, broad-minded conservatives and progressives get along fine and have intelligent conversations with each other. It's the closed-minded ones who don't.

The power of Twitter and other social media platforms

All of the incidents described at the beginning of this chapter involved Twitter campaigns calling out that the professors be punished and campus administrators reacting out of fear of bad publicity.

These social media campaigns come from a small minority of students and activists. The Pew Research Center reported that ten percent of Twitter users make 80 percent of the tweets. Of that ten percent, users are more likely to be younger, Democrats, politically active, more highly educated, and women. Studies have shown how Twitter movements can be controlled by a small but vocal minority unrepresentative of the larger population and how manipulative and corrosive this is to society and discourse. (Pew 2019) (Schlosser 2015) (Haidt 2019) (Zimmerman 2021) (O'Sullivan 2021) (Friedman 2018)

Writes McWhorter: "I think the spark for the current situation is perhaps more mundane than we'd like to think. I don't think that for some reason everybody went crazy. I don't think it's because of the president we happen to have in office [Trump]. I think it's social media. Social media, especially when you have it in your pocket in the form of the iPhone, allows bubbles of consensus to come together such that you can whip people up in a way that was not possible a generation before, or even ten years before." (Friedersdorf 2020)

University administrators as enablers

A key problem isn't the students, but that they are enabled by administrators. Undergrads are young. The school presidents, deans, and other administrators are supposed to be the adults in the room. However, administrators fear bad publicity and see students as paying customers to be catered to. (Handa 2021)

Samuel Abrams, a political science professor and board member of the Foundation for Individual Rights and Expression (FIRE), additionally argues that many administrators belong to an ideological monoculture, with over half having education degrees where they were schooled in the same pedagogical theories. (Abrams 2021) (Morey 2020)

Responding to MIT's cancellation of Dorian Abbot's lecture, MIT chemical engineering professor Bernhardt Trout wrote that "upper administration would clearly have just wanted to cancel Professor Abbot and be done with it and only spoke in defense of speech because of pushback from the community." (Sorey 2021)

This new culture is bad for community health

Communities that do not allow the expression of a diversity of thought, communities where people are intimidated into silence and unable to express their personal truths, are unhealthy and dysfunctional. Suppressing the diversity of ideas, debate, and the consideration of different ideas is bad in myriad ways. Forced conformity through shaming, punishment, and censorship should not be tolerated anywhere, but especially not in places of learning.

Illiberalism and intolerance undermine democracy

Healthy democracies require more than casting votes. Liberal democracy requires the freedoms and qualities of classical liberalism.

Democracy requires a well-informed voting public that is exposed to the diversity of views and information in society. Historian Eric Zuesse writes that "No democracy can survive censorship." The democracy advocacy organization Freedom House states, "Free speech and expression is the lifeblood of democracy, facilitating open debate, the proper consideration of diverse interests and perspectives, and the negotiation and compromise necessary for consensual policy decisions. Efforts to suppress nonviolent expression, far from ensuring peace and stability, can allow unseen problems to fester and erupt in far more dangerous forms." (Zuesse 2020)

The promotion and use of critical thinking are essential to a functioning democracy and free society. The critical thinking advocacy group Insight Assessment states: "Critical thinking promotes democracy. Like free and fair elections, critical thinking is essential for a healthy democracy. If voters are to make wise decisions, they must be both willing and able to think critically. We celebrate all who teach thinking. Teaching students how to examine issues, fair-mindedly, and how to analyze and evaluate diverging claims, thoughtfully, is vital to succeed as a free and informed democracy."

In her column "Democracy Needs Critical Thinking," Pulitzer Prize-winning journalist Cynthia Tucker writes, "There is little hope for this nation's democratic experiment if so many of our citizens cannot bear to hear fact-based beliefs that are different from their own. Shouldn't each of us be able to inspect our views to see if they hold up to the scrutiny of reason? If you can't bear to do that, there might be something suspect at the core of your beliefs." (Tucker 2021)

Democracy requires dissent and the platforming of a diversity of views. This should be obvious. Expulsion and punishment of dissenters are what totalitarian governments and fundamentalist religions do. Aung San Suu Kyi wrote, "To view the opposition as dangerous is to misunderstand the basic concepts of democracy. To oppress the opposition is to assault the very foundation of democracy."

Creating and maintaining a healthy democracy is the work of all. It is the responsibility of all to educate themselves and others, actively engage in critical thinking, and push back and speak out against illiberalism, dogmatism, and authoritarianism wherever they appear.

Dennis Chavez wrote, "Either we are all free, or we fail. Democracy must belong to all of us."

References

Abbot and Marinovic (2021), "The Diversity Problem on Campus," https://www.newsweek.com/diversity-problem-campus-opinion-1618419

Abbot, D. (2021), "MIT Abandons Its Mission. And Me," https://bariweiss.substack.com/p/mit-abandons-its-mission-and-me?s=r

Abrams, S. (2021), "How Did Universities Get So Woke? Look to the Administrators," https://www.newsweek.com/how-did-universities-get-so-woke-look-administrators-opinion-1635078

Agrawal, N. (2020), "Controversy over USC professor's use of Chinese word that sounds like racial slur in English," https://www.latimes.com/california/story/2020-09-05/usc-business-professor-controversy-chinese-word-english-slur

Aschwanden, C. (2020), "Why Hatred and 'Othering' of Political Foes Has Spiked to Extreme Levels," https://www.scientificamerican.com/article/why-hatred-and-othering-of-political-foes-has-spiked-to-extreme-levels/

Campbell & Manning (2018), *The Rise of Victimhood Culture*, Palgrave Macmillan

Churchill, C. (2020), "At Skidmore, curiosity might get you canceled," https://www.timesunion.com/news/article/Churchill-At-Skidmore-curiosity-might-get-you-15553968.php#photo-19749884

Demaske, C. (2020), "Critical Race Theory," https://www.mtsu.edu/first-amendment/article/1254/critical-race-theory

Deresiewicz, W. (2015), "We Aren't Raising Adults. We Are Breeding Very Excellent Sheep.," https://bariweiss.substack.com/p/we-arent-raising-adults-we-are-breeding?s=r

Friederdor, C. (2020), "Evidence That Conservative Students Really Do Self-Censor," https://www.theatlantic.com/ideas/archive/2020/02/evidence-conservative-students-really-do-self-censor/606559/

Friedersdorf, C. (2020), "The Rise of Victimhood Culture: A recent scholarly paper on 'microaggressions' uses them to chart the ascendance of a new moral code in American life," https://www.theatlantic.com/politics/archive/2015/09/the-rise-of-victimhood-culture/404794/

Friedman, D. (2019), "Nobody Should Listen to Twitter Mobs," https://quillette.com/2018/08/13/nobody-should-listen-to-twitter-mobs/

Gerson, J. (2014), "The Trouble with Teaching Rape Law," https://www.newyorker.com/news/news-desk/trouble-teaching-rape-law

Haidt and Lukianoff (2021), "How To Keep Your Corporation Out of the Culture War," https://www.persuasion.community/p/haidt-and-lukianoff-how-to-end-corporate?

Haidt, J. (2018), "How Colleges are Failing Kids," https://www.youtube.com/watch?v=uTYW1TOLJHE

Haidt, J. (2019), "Home of the Anxious and the Fragile," https://www.youtube.com/watch?v=jQcDw1r1lGw

Handa, S. (2021), "The Illiberalism in Our Institutions," https://www.persuasion.community/p/the-illiberalism-in-our-institutions?s=r

Harden, N. (2021), "As Colleges Moved Online to Combat the Pandemic, a Plague of Self-Censorship Raged On," https://www.realcleareducation.com/articles/2021/09/21/as_colleges_m oved_online_to_combat_the_pandemic_a_plague_of_self-censorship_raged_on_110636.html

Harris, J. (2022), "The Left Goes to War with Itself," https://www.politico.com/news/magazine/2022/06/23/the-new-battles-roiling-the-left-00041627

Harrison, T. (2021), "America Has a Scorn Problem," https://www.nytimes.com/2022/05/15/opinion/polarization-disagreement.html

HERI (2019), "The 2019 CIRP Freshman Survey," https://heri.ucla.edu

Inside Higher Ed (2020), "Varied Friendships Make Students More Tolerant," https://www.insidehighered.com/news/2019/10/15/college-students-friends-different-worldviews-are-more-tolerant-study-finds

Jacobson, W. (2021), "The Cruel and Unusual Punishment Of Prof. Jason Kilborn by U. Illinois-Chicago John Marshall Law School," https://legalinsurrection.com/2021/12/the-cruel-and-unusual-punishment-of-prof-jason-kilborn-by-u-illinois-chicago-john-marshall-law-school/

Klein, G. (2021), "Why I Am Suing UCLA.I refused to discriminate against my students. Then the problems began," https://bariweiss.substack.com/p/why-i-am-suing-ucla?s=r

Krylov A (2021), "The Peril of Politicizing Science," https://pubs.acs.org/doi/full/10.1021/acs.jpclett.1c01475

Krylov A & Tanzman J (2021), "Academic Ideologues Are Corrupting STEM. The Silent Liberal Majority Must Fight Back", https://quillette.com/2021/12/18/scientists-must-gain-the-courage-to-oppose-the-politicization-of-their-disciplines

Leef, G. (2018), "Victimhood Culture Engulfs Our Campuses," https://www.nationalreview.com/corner/victimhood-culture-left-college-campuses-engulfed/

Lehman, C. (2018), "Understanding Victimhood Culture: An Interview with Bradley Campbell and Jason Manning," https://quillette.com/2018/05/17/understanding-victimhood-culture-interview-bradley-campbell-jason-manning/

Loury, G. and Haidt, J. (20220, "Jonathan Haidt—After Babel," https://glennloury.substack.com/p/jonathan-haidt-after-babel#details

Loury, G. and McWhorter, J. (2022), "Policing Joe Rogan," https://www.youtube.com/watch?v=oC7CCqqPOyo

McGahan, J. (2020), "How a Mild-Mannered USC Professor Accidentally Ignited Academia's Latest Culture War," https://www.lamag.com/citythinkblog/usc-professor-slur/

Morey, A. (2022), "St. Olaf ousts faculty director of institute dedicated to bringing controversial speakers to campus—because speakers caused controversy," https://www.thefire.org/st-olaf-ousts-faculty-director-of-institute-dedicated-to-bringing-controversial-speakers-to-campus-because-speakers-caused-controversy/

Morey, A. (2020), "UCLA reinstated Gordon Klein. Who will reinstate his reputation?", https://www.thefire.org/ucla-reinstated-gordon-klein-who-will-reinstate-his-reputation/

Morey, A. (2020) "Sarah Lawrence's Samuel Abrams, viewpoint diversity scholar who defied cancellation, joins FIRE's Advisory Council," https://www.thefire.org/sarah-lawrences-samuel-abrams-viewpoint-diversity-scholar-who-defied-cancellation-joins-fires-advisory-council/

MTC (2016), "A Conversation with Jonathan Haidt: 'Most people are Horrified by what's going on in the universities,'" https://www.mindingthecampus.org/2016/02/03/a-conversation-with-jonathan-haidt/

Nakagome, Y. (2020), "USC professor placed on leave after speaking Chinese should be reinstated," https://dailytrojan.com/2020/09/22/usc-professor-placed-on-leave-after-speaking-chinese-should-be-reinstated/

O'Sullivan, D. (2021), "The Mathematics of Twitter Mobs," https://areomagazine.com/2021/07/07/the-mathematics-of-twitter-mobs/

Paikin, S. (2019), "Home of the Anxious and the Fragile," https://www.youtube.com/watch?v=jQcDw1r1lGw

Pew (2019), "Sizing Up Twitter Users," https://www.pewresearch.org/internet/2019/04/24/sizing-up-twitter-users/

PRI (2019), "Why Are Teachers Mostly Liberal?", https://www.pacificresearch.org/why-are-teachers-mostly-liberal/

Rampell, C. (2016), "Liberal intolerance is on the rise on America's college campuses," https://www.washingtonpost.com/opinions/liberal-but-not-tolerant-on-the-nations-college-campuses/2016/02/11/0f79e8e8-d101-11e5-88cd-753e80cd29ad_story.html

Sachs, J. (2019), "The 'Campus Free Speech Crisis' Ended Last Year," https://www.niskanencenter.org/the-campus-free-speech-crisis-ended-last-year/

Schlosser, E. (2015), "I'm a liberal professor, and my liberal students terrify me," https://www.vox.com/2015/6/3/8706323/college-professor-afraid

Small, A. (2021), "Who Comes After Doran Abbot?", https://www.insidehighered.com/views/2021/11/08/dorian-abbot-case-could-have-broad-negative-repercussions-opinion

Soave, R. (2020), "Students Demand Skidmore College Fire an Art Professor for Observing a Pro-Cop Rally," https://reason.com/2020/09/11/skidmore-college-david-petrson-students-cop-rally-cancel/

Sorey, R. (2021), "Princeton director blasts MIT for 'chilling' decision to cancel professor's lecture, thousands log on to hear prof's science research," https://www.bostonherald.com/2021/10/21/princeton-director-blasts-mit-for-chilling-decision-to-cancel-professors-lecture-thousands-log-on-to-hear-profs-science-research/

Stevens, S. (2020), "Faculty report from University of Southern California's business school reveals deep concerns about academic freedom," https://www.thefire.org/faculty-report-from-university-of-southern-californias-business-school-reveals-deep-concerns-about-academic-freedom-a-recent-internal-report-from-the-university-of-southern-california/

Tarico, V. (2021), "An Excess of Woke Thinking May Harm Mental Health or Relationships," https://valerietarico.com/2021/12/15/an-excess-of-woke-thinking-may-harm-mental-health-or-relationships/

Troy, T. (2019), "The Long and Winding Road to Campus Illiberalism," https://www.discoursemagazine.com/culture-and-society/2021/11/30/the-long-and-winding-road-to-campus-illiberalism/

Tucker, C. (2021), "Democracy needs critical thinking," timesunion.com/opinion/article/Cynthia-Tucker-Democracy-needs-critical-thinking-16603965.php

UCLA (2019), "The Faculty Code of Conduct," https://www.ucop.edu/academic-personnel-programs/_files/apm/apm-015.pdf

Volokh, E. (2020), "Letter from USC Marshall School of Business Alumni About the 'Neige' / Prof. Greg Patton Controversy," https://reason.com/volokh/2020/09/07/letter-from-usc-marshall-school-of-business-alumni-about-the-neige-prof-greg-patton-controversy/.

WebMD (2022), "What is Victim Mentality?", https://www.webmd.com/mental-health/what-is-a-victim-mentality

Zimmerman, J. (2021), "On American campuses, students are biting their tongues," https://www.inquirer.com/opinion/commentary/students-free-speech-college-campus-censorship-20210930.html

Zuesse, E. (2020), "Censorship Is the Way that Any Dictatorship—and NO Democracy—Functions," strategic-culture.org/news/2020/02/15/censorship-is-way-that-any-dictatorship-no-democracy-functions/

13 Intolerance and Illiberalism in Unitarian Universalism

As described in Chapter 2, Unitarian Universalism has long been one of the most liberal and tolerant churches. It has upheld individual paths and personal theological choices, freedom of expression, and the democratic process. Unlike the congregations in top-down religions such as Catholicism, UU congregations are independent and self-determining.

However, following illiberal trends in other institutions, the national UU leadership has been taken over by zealous self-proclaimed radicals who are trying to transform UU into an illiberal, top-town church. (VUU 2017)

The worst excesses of woke culture you can think of, as described in Chapters 10-12, are now found in the national UU: Dogmatism, religious-like fanaticism and self-righteousness, racial essentialism and neo-racism, censorship, call-out and cancel culture, victimhood culture, ideological language and language policing, expectations of ideological and political conformity, punishment and even expulsion of perceived heretics.

John McWhorter's 2021 *New York Times* best seller *Woke Racism: How a New Religion Has Betrayed Black America* cites the current national UU as an exemplar of the new intolerance that is found within the far left. Elsewhere, McWhorter writes, "Unitarianism has been all but taken over in many places by modern antiracist theology, forcing the resignation of various ministers and other figures. The new faith also manifests itself in objections to what its adherents process as dissent." (McWhorter 2020)

In his sermon on resignation from UU, lifelong UU Chris Brimmer said, "The Church writ large has become a labyrinth of language traps, purity tests, and half-baked ideas that have become sacred cows that are above critical examination. I cannot be the member of a church that is now just like any other church, with dogma above questioning and a hierarchy that conducts heresy trials." (Brimmer 2022)

UU Minister Rev. Munro Sickafoose wrote, "It's about what I see as the merging of an extreme political ideology into Unitarian Universalism, and its transformation into a reactionary religious movement that exhibits all the hallmarks of fundamentalism." (Sickafoose 2019)

The following are some examples of what is going on:

Unilaterally declaring UU to be a "white supremacy culture" that must be dismantled

In what a UU minister called a "coup" by "reactionaries," radicals took over the UUA board and unilaterally declared one of the most historically progressive churches irredeemably racist and a "white supremacy culture" that must be dismantled. The UUA adopted Tema Okun's dubious ideas of a monolithic white culture and promotes Robin DiAngelo's neo-racist and racial essentialist ideology that all whites are inherently and eternally racist and oppressors and that racial minorities are inherently oppressed. (Sickafoose 2019) (Pine 2019) (Hewitt and de la Fuente 2021) (UUA 2017) (UUA 2021)

The new Original Sin of UUs having been born morally corrupt due to the color of their skin defies UU's rejection of original sin and upends the church's first principle of "the inherent worth and dignity of every person." UU is full of ex-Catholics who rejected such a guilt and shame upbringing.

Echoing many UUs, congregant Nancy Haldeman wrote to her Oregon congregation's board, "I consider myself a liberal, a moderate Democrat, and someone seeking racial equality throughout my life. I was in shock when I heard all of us, white congregants, referred to as white supremacists and racists from the pulpit! I have been attending the congregation for over 27 years and have never heard anything so outrageous in my life! I attend church to be uplifted and inspired. I do not intend to be labeled in a negative way."

Economic inequality expert Dick Burkhart wrote in a letter to the UUA President, "I am not aware of even a single documented example of a current UU practice grounded in a belief in white racial superiority. Instead, we have a multitude of evidence-free accusations of 'white supremacy culture,' justified only by Orwellian redefinitions that are so murky that literally any artifact of European culture could be so labeled (even "2+2=4", believe it or not)."

Of equal concern are all the UUs who are so willing to self-flagellate and submit to what is, as a UU minister put it, a "sin-and-salvation approach to social justice." A UU said, "We're all going to change our way of thinking." That struck me as something you would hear from a member of a cult. (Holt 2021)

Adopting a dogma

In a church advertising itself as having no creed, the UUA unilaterally declared an extreme version of critical race theory as a "theological mandate" for all congregations and UUs. Theological mandate is another term for dogma or creed. (UUA 2020)

It promotes and attempts to enforce extreme identity politics and CRT ideas such as that reason, logic, meritocracy, freedom of expression, and science are oppressive of minorities. People are to be viewed and weighed primarily by the color of their skin and other immutable characteristics. The subjective views of minorities are to be taken as unquestionable truth-telling. Any disparity in outcome is classified as necessarily due to racism. Any disagreement or dissent from whites is deemed "racist," "fragility," "upholding of white supremacy," and "harm." (UUA 2018) (Hewitt & de la Fuente 2021) (UUA 2021) (UUA 2017) (UUA 2020)

UU congregant Donna Templeton wrote, "What drew me to UU is the freedom of thought, the sharing of ideas, the being free to differ and debate while holding each other with respect. What drew me to UU is that it eschews dogma, or at least it used to. I fear that is no longer true. If the only way we, as UUs, are allowed to think about and deal with racism and, by extension, anything else we are concerned with is by following the edicts of CRT, how is that not dogma?"

Attempting to remove liberalism from liberal religion

Following CRT, the UUA and UU leaders have pushed against liberalism and religious liberalism. The UUA has promoted that individualism and "allergy to authority" are the "errors of UUs."

Two UUA leaders stated that the central UU tenet of freedom of belief is a "throwback." Jim Aikin writes, "Our national organization, the UUA, has been taken over by a group who are not committed in any way to individual liberty. They feel it's old-fashioned." (Muir 2013) (VUU 2018) (5th Principle Project 2022) (Mattis 2022) (Aikin 2022)

Removing liberalism and freedom of belief from UU is like removing Jesus from Christianity.

Control of information

The national UU has worked to tightly control information. Under the direction of the UUA, *UU World* magazine has ceased to publish letters to the editor and has stated it will only publish views that support the new orthodoxy. (Walton 2019) (Wells 2019) (5th Principle Project 2020)

One longtime minister called *UU World* "an ideological propaganda organ," and another called it "Pravda." Former *UU World* columnist Jeffrey A. Lockwood wrote, "The current direction of the UUA is divisive, accusatory, destructive, and contrary to UU principles. Censorship is fundamentally inimical to our religious traditions and values."

UU national leaders and ministers under the new orthodoxy have told other ministers and congregants not to read books of which they do not approve, and ministers themselves have said they refuse to read certain books. Dissenting views have been censored and dissenters removed from public forums at the General Assembly. A racial justice group that promotes a Martin Luther King Jr./John Lewis style of social justice that works to unite races in social justice work was banned from exhibiting at General Assembly because it does not adhere to the UUA's strict

CRT dogma. A dissenting group promoting democracy was not allowed to promote its book at GA. (Trudeau 2019) (Pine 2019) (Aikin 2019) (Cain 2019) (Aikin 2021) (UUMUAC 2022)

Suppressing the diversity of views, punishing and even expelling dissenters

As UUA sees its views as unilateral and dogma, dissent and countering views are not only not allowed but shut down and punished. Dissent and the expression of other perspectives from both laity and ministers are often met with public attacks and dissenters are accused of being "racist" and "upholding of white supremacy." As described in Chapter 11, this is meant to intimidate and stop debate.

Rev. Cynthia Cain writes, "UUs everywhere, but particularly clergy and particularly on social media, are afraid to speak their truth. Their fear is due to their perception that not only will they be shamed, shouted down, and piled upon metaphorically, but that they may actually lose their standing with our association and consequently their livelihoods. This I know for certain." (Cain 2019)

Rev. Rick Davis wrote: "It's a frightening time for many today who feel as though the slightest, innocent slip can result in loss of livelihood and reputation." (Davis 2020)

Following the new UUA orthodoxy, many newly ordained ministers have worked to stifle dissent in congregations. They often platform only the UUA-approved agenda and censor, punish, and even expel dissenting congregants. Congregants have been publicly called out for questioning the orthodoxy and even recommending the reading of unapproved books. A few ministers have promoted the idea that dissenting congregants should be "re-educated" or asked to leave. One UU leader said that older liberal congregants should change their way of thinking or leave UU. (VUU 2020)

Wrote one congregant: "Many congregations are more afraid of becoming split apart than they are afraid of falling under the distortions formulated by the current UUA junta. This fear drives many church leaders towards silencing outspoken voices. I have already been seriously, and formally, threatened."

In an open letter, longtime ministers quit the Unitarian Universalist Ministers Association (UUMA) in part expressing their "alarm at the growing dogmatism and intolerance in our UUMA. . . . Despite (for many of us) long years of cherished ministerial collegiality, the UUMA has become for us an inhospitable place and an embarrassment. As it has been made clear that genuine dialog on the new orthodoxy will not be tolerated in our ministerial association, we cannot in good faith continue our association with it." (UU Ministers 2020)

Longtime UU minister Rev. Alex Holt wrote in an open resignation letter to the UUMA: "Does the UUMA even care about those who have raised their voices critiquing what feels like a sin-and-salvation approach to justice? I don't know the answers, but I do know that I cannot in good conscience be part of an organization that speaks of accountability and covenant on one hand but punishes those who disagree on the other." (Holt 2021)

Suppressing minority voices

Despite its sloganeering, the new UUA political paradigm is not about centering the voices of minorities but a particular narrow ideology. Like-minded whites Tema Okun, Robin DiAngelo and

Susan Frederick-Gray are exalted, while heterodox minorities such as John McWhorter, Irshad Manji, and Bari Weiss are dismissed, undermined, and ad hominem attacked.

This is why all of the UUA's and *UU World's* rhetoric about "centering the voices of minority groups" is false. It is about centering those who agree with a particular narrow ideological and political paradigm. It is bigoted, ignorant, and condescending to minorities to say that minorities think or should think only one way. (Journal of Free Black Thought 2021)

Censuring a minister for asking questions and asking for dialogue

Rev. Richard Trudeau is a UU minister emeritus, a retired professor and author of books on liberal religion and UU history. In a Unitarian Universalists Ministers Association (UUMA) colleagues forum, he asked questions about UU trends, including the UUA's use of a non-standard definition of racism that had caused communication problems among UUs. He also said that many UUs seemed to be motivated by a sense of "white guilt." He asked if there could be a space for ministers to discuss these and other topics. (Trudeau 2019) (Trudeau 2022)

These are perfectly reasonable questions that have not only been asked by laity but by the black intellectuals McWhorter, Shelby Steele, and Coleman Hughes. (Steele 2006) (McWhorter 2021)

For asking these questions and asking for a space for ministers to discuss them, Trudeau was expelled from the forum and given a letter of censure copied to all ministers saying he had caused "harm," even though no one had expressed to him that they felt they had been harmed.

Trudeau wrote the UUMA that the censure "undercuts a foundational Unitarian Universalist value, viz., each person's right to ask questions," "civil society's freedom of speech," and UU's own principles. The UUMA never responded.

The excommunication of a minister for writing a book

Rev. Dr. Todd Eklof is the minister at the Unitarian Universalist Church of Spokane, Washington. A supporter of liberal religion and freedom of speech, he wrote a short 2019 book titled *The Gadfly Papers: Three Inconvenient Essays by One Pesky Minister*. It is described as "a collection of three essays written by Rev. Dr. Todd F. Eklof about the negative impacts the emerging culture of Political Correctness, Safetyism, and Identitarianism is having on America's most liberal religion."

Eklof's book was banned at General Assembly, the annual national convention. He was publicly censured and expelled from the UUA. In the new style, he was publicly smeared, the book being called "harmful" and subjected to the usual ad hominem string of insults of "racist," "sexist," "homophobic," "ableist," "transphobic." etc. This is even though most readers who have read the book are mystified at what might be considered harmful in it, and even though Eklof is a longtime progressive social justice and gay and lesbian rights activist. (Kentucky Insider 2007) (Fortune 2005)

Jim Aikin wrote, "The book was attacked as being 'ableist' and 'transphobic,' among other terms, even though there wasn't a word in it that could possibly be interpreted in those terms," and "It's clear that most of them hadn't read the book before they attacked it." (Aikin 2022)

A longtime minister wrote to other ministers, "[T]his is about the authoritarian turn the UUA has taken and its immediate move to destroy the reputations and careers of anyone they disagree with, usually by claiming or insinuating they are racists."

Immediately after the book was first distributed at General Assembly, over 300 white ministers signed a public letter condemning the book and the minister even though most of the ministers had not read it. A top UUA official wrote for other ministers to add their signatures to the letter and told them not to read the book.

Rev. Richard Trudeau said, "These ministers, over 300 of them, signed this letter within 24 hours. The book distribution had only begun 24 hours previously, so almost certainly the vast majority of these ministers hadn't even read the book. They condemn a book they had not even read. This seems so otherworldly that UU ministers could do that." (Trudeau 2022)

Book banning and punishing a minister for dissent was shocking to many UU laity and many ministers, as they are the complete opposite of UU tradition. (Wells 2019)

When the UUMA posted its censure of Eklof the following were replies by ministers. (UUMA 2019):

> "In 1553, Michael Servetus was burned at the stake for writing and speaking his heretical ideas. I guess we do it differently today."

> "This is a shameful document that will be remembered as a low point in our history! Orthodoxy by fiat is not the UU way. This censure does not represent me and many other ministers—and I believe the signers are in violation of UUMA covenants in ways far more egregious than anything Rev. Eklof did."

"I've not been a member for years, but the UUMA is now good and dead to me. The signatories can (to put it nicely) get lost. I'm embarrassed for them; they should be ashamed of themselves." (Wells 2019)

In his essay "Dogmatism and Fanaticism in UU," Rev. Mark Gallagher wrote, "About 10% of the signers are ministerial candidates or aspirants, and many more are new in ministry. I believe that in this process we are teaching our junior colleagues to join in condemning one another casually and unreflectively, the very definition of fanaticism." (Gallagher 2019)

National leaders have disingenuously tried to paint it that Eklof wasn't punished and expelled because of his dissent or book writing but because he didn't follow proper procedures. However, clear-eyed UUs know exactly why he was censured and expelled.

Trudeau wrote, "These organizations have claimed procedural irregularities as the reasons for their actions, but upon close inspection, I don't find that any of their explanations hold water."

Chris Brimmer said, "Then came the defrocking. I'm not going to play word games on this not being a defrocking, that it was a loss of professional certification or a withdrawal of professional credentials, blah, blah, blah. If it walks like a duck, quacks like a duck, it's a duck. He was asked to put his head in the guillotine of a theological drumhead tribunal and when he refused they shot him. Nothing speaks to me more of the fundamental dishonesty of the whole process than when the Good Officer acting on Rev. Eklof's behalf, Rev. Rick Davis, has found himself the subject of professional discipline when he defended Elkof instead of shepherding him into the public admission of heresy that they were looking for and [that] would justify their actions." (Brimmer 2021)

As mentioned by Brimmer, Eklof's Good Officer, Rev. Rick Davis, was removed from the Good Officer program for advocating for Eklof. A Good Officer's job is to act as a proverbial public defender for the minister they represent. Davis afterward called the whole process a "kangaroo court" and "a setup to provide a predetermined outcome." He referred to the new UUMA's discipline procedures as "truly Kafka-esque." (Davis 2020)

The answer is to read the book and judge for yourself. You likely will be one of the many who, while they may or may not agree with all of the author's points, cannot find a single line that is offensive.

Russian dissident poet Joseph Brodsky said, "There are worse crimes than burning books. One of them is not reading them."

Dogmatic seminaries producing dogmatic ministers

The two UU seminaries have become dogmatic, teaching seminary students what to think rather than how to think. A graduate said that "CRT is now pounded into the students."

A longtime UU minister wrote, "I think the biggest danger to local congregations is the takeover of seminaries and the credentialing of clergy. Newly minted clergy are overwhelmingly indoctrinated and, if they aren't, they will have a hard time being accepted as UU clergy."

Having experienced learned, broad-minded UU and interfaith ministers in the past, I have been shocked at how closed-minded, dogmatic, and bigoted are many new ministers. There are many approaches to social and racial justice work, but they have been taught there is only the one acceptable one.

Trudeau says that many ministers do not think it is their job to serve the congregations that pay them, and that they are really working for the UUA. He said, "They feel it's their job to push the UUA's point of view on every congregation they serve. And there are lots of ministers who don't agree with what the UUA is pushing but they don't want to get in trouble with the UUA. There's a lot of problems of integrity. A lot of ministers have a problem with integrity." (Trudeau 2022)

In his paper "How the UUA Manufactures Consent," UU Minister Rev. Gary Kowalski wrote, "The UUA Board appoints over two-thirds of the members of the Ministerial Fellowship Committee. Seminarians and smart young clergy in preliminary fellowship know they must pass a litmus test to receive their punch card to practice ministry. Consciously or unconsciously, they understand they must not rock the boat." He also writes, "By weeding out outliers, the Board grooms the next generation of trusted functionaries to serve on its endless committees and run the bureaucracy." (Kowalski 2020)

Undermining democracy

In its very principles, Unitarian Universalism is premised on the right of conscience and democratic processes. The UUA has had well-publicized "UU the Vote" campaigns to promote getting out the vote in the national elections across the country. However, the UUA hypocritically works to dismantle the pillars of democracy and create an anti-democracy culture and theology within UU. (UUA 2019) (Beyer 2019)

The 2009 UUA-Board-commissioned Fifth Principle Task Force Report to the UUA stated that General Assembly is "dramatically broken" and, "The future of our UU movement can ill-afford to continue the ways of faux democracy and unaccountable representation that have characterized associational governance, including the content and process of the General Assembly." (Fifth Principle Task Report 2009)

These problems have been acknowledged by the UUA and the Commission on Institutional Change (COIC). Yet the UUA Board of Trustees and President are elected by only 1.oent of the UU members. The loss of representational districts gutted UU representational democracy, and the report says it is "questionable how well the delegate body represents and is accountable to member congregations." (Fifth Principle Task Report 2009) (UUA 2020)

Beyond these acknowledged problems, the national UU leadership does more fundamental things to undermine and dismantle the very culture and practice of democracy. These include censorship and control of information, suppression of dissent and expulsion of heterodox thinkers, and trying to stifle freedom of speech and open debate.

Wrote one longtime UU, "This is a serious problem. There are thousands of UUs who have no idea that there is a controversy. Of course, the main way that UUs are contacted is through institutional communications. These channels are completely unwilling to host discussions of the problems."

Another person wrote: "If you don't think a certain way and conform in belief and speech, you must be ostracized and shut down. It is nascent authoritarianism and a symptom of social and political infection. It is as much a threat to democracy as rightwing extremism."

In "How the UUA Manufacturers Consent," Rev. Kowalski details how power was consolidated in the Board of Trustees, making the UUA centrally controlled by a small, insular group. Kowalski writes, "The switch to policy governance ended by making our Association less democratic, less diverse and more centrally controlled," "General Assembly is largely a spectacle where delegates wave their yellow ballots on cue," and "When given unchecked authority, automatic ascent to electoral victory, and the power to judge, punish, and control the livelihoods of others who stand in their way, while cloaking themselves in a mantle of moral purity, even the best human beings succumb to their worst instincts." (Kowalski 2020)

Since Kowalski's essay, the Board of Trustees has instituted rules to make it even more difficult if not practically impossible for an outsider to run for President, and has said that all candidates should be ideologically vetted by the Board. (Gadfly Pages 2022) (Mattis 2022) (UUA BOT 2022)

Miles Fidelman, a professional policy analyst and systems architect, said, "Nothing new here, for any student of history and organizational dynamics. Pretty standard practice for any cabal. What's worse, is they generally think they're doing the right thing, for the right reasons. Also, not at all surprising is how easily folks go along with it. Google 'useful idiots.'"

The UUA has become a textbook example of illiberal democracy, employing anti-democratic methods used by countries such as Russia, Belarus, and Hungary.

This also points to a dishonesty in the UUA and national leadership. Any organization that proclaims, "We support democracy," while simultaneously undermining it, or says, "We are a non-creed religion," while trying to impose a creed, is fundamentally dishonest.

Becoming a mirror-image of politically partisan Christian Evangelical churches

A UU recently posted the 2022 Atlantic magazine article *How Politics Poisoned the Evangelical Church* by journalist and preacher's son Tim Alberta. The article documents how many Evangelical Christian congregations became overtly Pro-Trump with the Preachers preaching far right politics and political conspiracy theories from the pulpit. The UU poster said how much it reminded him of the current national UU. (Alberta 2022)

Social activism has always been part of UU. However, the national UU has become what often resembles an extremist leftist Political Action Committee. I counted more than half the articles on UU World's web homepage as being overtly political, and a visitor to the UUA's Facebook page might not guess it's the page of a religion. The extreme positions (abolish the police and prisons, extremist social theories, supporting riots) are presented as papal bulls with the implication that UUs who disagree are "racist," and "upholders of white supremacy." The "UU the Vote" campaigns come across as a PAC to get Democrats elected.

Most UUs are liberals not radicals, and many UUs attend a congregation for spirituality and Sunday service as an oasis from social media and cable news. Inserting radical politics into any community is certain to cause strife.

A man looking for a liberal church and spiritual community wrote, "I left when I came to realize that it is little more than a left-wing political advocacy group masquerading as a religion."

Victimhood culture and infantilizing UUs

UU leaders, the seminaries, many ministers, and activists have adopted the victimhood culture and identity politics caste system described in Chapter 12. Using the most extreme neo-racist and racially essentialist interpretations of CRT and identity politics, they began "centering" and "decentering" and even segregating congregants based on race. Audiences and groups at the annual General Assembly are now racially segregated. They have tried to make UU congregations into safe spaces where people should be protected from heterodox ideas and words. (UUA NER 2019) (VUU 2018) (McCardle 2019) (Harper 2021)

One example that has stood out to me is the national UU's scrubbing UU language of supposedly harmful words. It has removed "ableist" words such as see, hear, walk and stand. It changed its slogan from "Standing on the Side of Love" to "Siding with Love" because the word stand was deemed "ableist" and harmful to people with disabilities.

Not only do I have mental disorders, but my research is in part in neurodiversity and people with mental disorders, and I am in the Disabilities Division of the American Philosophical Association. I know that this removal of "ableist" language is counter to the views of most people with disabilities.

The majority of disabled people find not only condescending but offensive the extreme sanitizing of language. A UU friend who is quadriplegic and permanently in a wheelchair said that removing the word stand from "Standing on the Side of Love" was the most idiotic thing he'd heard of, and he will continue to say "stand." A judge and former disability rights lawyer is confined to a motorized wheelchair and says with a smile, "I'm going out for a walk." He said this excessive sanitation of language is promoted by people who mean well but do not understand what most people with disabilities think and want.

Most people with disabilities understand, appreciate, and use metaphors. Despite what the UUA promotes these days, being disabled doesn't mean being stupid or wanting to be considered as a child.

As is standard procedure these days, the UUA has designed church policy from the viewpoint of a fringe, hypersensitive element within a minority population. Extremists are proxies only for themselves, and you don't design communities based on the most easily offended.

These have been just several examples, with recommended further reading provided at the end of this chapter.

How UU is susceptible to dogmatism

Retired UU Minister Rev. Dr. Davidson Loehr and UU author Jim Aikin have written that UU is susceptible to falling for political dogmatism because it has no core theological belief. (Loehr 2005)

Aikin writes, "This way of looking at it goes a long way to explaining why the UUA has been taken over by the toxic anti-racist cult. As I see it . . . antiracism found a ready home in Unitarian-Universalism because UUism isn't a religion at all. We have the trappings of religion—ministers, hymn-singing, passing the basket, all that good stuff. But there are no core beliefs in UUism. Prior to the merger, Unitarianism had not had any core beliefs for a hundred years. It had drifted into rational humanism, so it was fertile soil in which the bad seed could take root. The nice people running the UUA wanted to be a religion; they thought they were a religion already; but something was missing from their experience of religious feeling." (Aikin 2022)

In his essay "The High Church of Wokeism," educator Joseph Keegin wrote: "The German political theorist Carl Schmitt famously said that all modern political thought occurs through 'secularized theological concepts.' Unitarian Universalism does it backwards: Instead of secularizing theology into politics, it has attempted to consecrate liberal politics into a theology." (Keegian 2021)

Division and strife

In Chapter 7 I wrote that a key criticism of dogmatic critical race theory and the ideas of Kendi and DiAngelo is that they are counterproductive to racial justice progress because they divide rather than unite people in the cause.

The current UU leadership's authoritarian, illiberal approach to social justice has caused division and strife in Unitarian Universalist congregations and groups across the country. Congregations have split, longtime congregants have quit UU or cut their pledges, many young ministers have met pushback, and there has been a record number of ministers "mutually separating" from their congregations. There has been talk of a split in the church and the forming of alternatives to the Unitarian Universalist Association and the UUMA. (Aikin 2022)

In mid-2022, the UUA reported the largest drop in membership and the largest drop in the number of congregations in the church's history. The report shows that there are now the fewest ever UU congregations. The previous UUA report in 2020 showed the largest drop in membership in twenty-three years. A longtime minister said he expected the drop to continue, in particular at large congregations. (UUA 2020) (UUA 2022)

One congregant wrote, "The passionate adherents to this framework are sowing division within UU communities and needlessly pushing away people who are natural allies in a struggle every UU supports." Another said that due to the divisiveness, alienation, and backlash it has produced amongst UUs, the national UU's heavy-handed methods have set racial justice back in UU and many congregations. (Westside 2021)

This should have been predicted. Illiberalism and liberalism, freedom of speech and suppression of freedom of speech, are mutually exclusive. Trying to unilaterally impose a creed onto a non-creed church will necessarily cause strife. Even national leaders acknowledged that most UU laity are liberals, not radicals. A veteran UU minister once compared trying to get congregants to agree to a single thing to herding cats. (VUU 2018)

That this has caused such strife and division in what is perhaps the country's most left-leaning church shows how poorly such methodology will work in the broader country. UU is spending more time on ideological purity tests and circular firing squads than on productive social justice work.

My mother is a longtime civil rights activist and Title IX pioneer. She quit UU in 2019, explaining, "UU is no longer UU. It has become like other religions. I don't like how the UUA tries to control what are supposed to be independent congregations, and I don't go for dogma. UU has also become mean." Pushing out progressives such as her damages UU and UU's social justice work.

The UUA's policy positions are so extreme, eccentric, and strident that they have diminished UU's position and effectiveness in the wider world. When UUA leaders stridently stick to "abolish the police" and ad hominem attack even progressives who disagree, they're making UU into what the outside world will view as a fringe, eccentric nonentity. UU will no longer be an effective agent of change or the unifying force for the broader society that it aspires to be. Many minorities say that extremist positions and actions not only don't represent their views but hurt the cause.

Rev. Munro Sickafoose wrote, "If we become a shrill and illiberal faith, I believe we are doomed to irrelevance." (Sickafoose 2019)

University of Chicago religion critic Jerry Coyne praised UU (see Chapter 2), but recently wrote, "Since UU is one of the few 'religions' that I haven't criticized strongly, as it is nondogmatic, liberal, and (I thought) charitable, I was truly disappointed to see it turning into The Evergreen Church of Perpetual Offense." (Coyne 2019)

How this will all play out in Unitarian Universalism only time will tell. However, the plummeting membership, dissolving congregations, and increasing strife do not point to a pleasant or productive future.

Recommended Further Reading

- 'Standing on the Side of Power' by Rev. Munro Sickafoose (Reprinted in Appendix)
- 'I Vs. We' by Jim Aikin (Reprinted in Appendix)
- Book: *Used to Be UU: The Systematic Attack on UU Liberalism* by Casper & Kiskel
- Book: *The Gadfly Affair: A 21st Century Heretic's Excommunication from America's Most Liberal Religion* by Dr. Rev. Todd Eklof

References

Aikin, J. (2019), "Shut Up! You're Not Liberal Enough!", https://midiguru.wordpress.com/2019/06/24/shut-up-youre-not-liberal-enough/

Aikin, J. (2021), "Something Wicked This Way Comes," https://midiguru.wordpress.com/2021/03/24/something-wicked-this-way-comes-2/

Aikin, J. (2022), "McWhorter's Book on Woke Antirsacism," https://midiguru.wordpress.com/2022/01/25/woke-joke/

Aikin J (2022), "I vs. We", Appendix

Alberta T (2022), "How Politics Poisoned the Evangelical Church", https://www.theatlantic.com/magazine/archive/2022/06/evangelical-church-pastors-political-radicalization/629631/

Brimmer, C. (2022), "Why I Resigned," https://www.facebook.com/chris.brimmer/posts/10220807490683244

Cain, C. (2019), "I Love you . . . Now Change!," https://ajerseygirlinkentucky.blogspot.com/search?q=eklof

Coyne, J. (2019), "UU Minister Flagellate Themselves," https://whyevolutionistrue.com/2019/09/07/unitarian-universalist-ministers-flagellate-themselves-and-the-church-for-one-bad-apple-assert-that-logic-and-reason-are-tools-of-white-supremacy/

Davis, R. (2020), "Good Officers Account," https://uusalem.org/wp-content/uploads/2020/12/Good-Offices-Account-Chapter-for-Fifth-Principle-Book-Project.pdf

Devilhead Reflects (2020), "The Debacle of GA '19: What Rev. Todd Eklof and the Spokane Church Can Do," http://devilheadreflects.blogspot.com/2020/02/the-debacle-of-ga-19-what-rev-todd.html

Disaffected Colleagues (2020), "We Quit Letter," https://uusalem.org/wp-content/uploads/2020/12/We-Quit-UUMA-letter-as-delivered.pdf

Fifth Principle Project (2022), "Meeting with Article II Study Commission," https://fifthprincipleproject.org/2022/06/15/meeting-with-article-ii-study-commission

Fortune, C. (2005), "An unlikely ally, Rev. Eklof rallies for marriage equality," http://www,pridesource.com/article/15185/

The Gadfly Pages, May 2022, https://centerforartifactstudiesorg.files.wordpress.com/2022/07/gadflypages5-22.pdf

Gallagher, M. (2019), "Dogmatism and Fanaticism in UU," https://trulyopenmindsandhearts.blog/2019/10/28/dogmatism-and-fanaticism-in-uu/

Gray-Frederick S (2019), "The Power of We", https://www.uuworld.org/articles/president-spring-2019

Hewitt, E. & de la Fuente, J. (2021), "Dismantling White Supremacy Culture in Worship," https://www.uua.org/worship/lab/dismantling-white-supremacy-culture-worship

Holt, A. (2021), "Another UU Minister Resigns from the UUMA," https://fifthprincipleproject.org/2021/07/29/another-uu-minister-resigns-from-the-uuma/

Journal of Free Black Thought (2021), "Introducing the Journal of Free Black Thought: A celebration of black viewpoint diversity," https://freeblackthought.substack.com/p/coming-soon

Keegin, J. (2021), "The High Church of Wokeism," https://www.tabletmag.com/sections/news/articles/beacon-unitarians-joseph-keegin

Kentuckyinsider (2005),"Todd Eklof Fired by Kentucky Farm Bureau for Supporting Gays," https://www.youtube.com/watch?v=A1yLCKtmBRM

Kowalski G (2020), "How the UUA Manufactures Consent", https://docs.google.com/document/d/1CM7jlpXTCQUdGfC_y5n4NXWRCQ01LvsJqueZNmDxyfc/

Loehr, D. (2005), "Why Unitarian Universalism is Dying," https://files.meadville.edu/files/resources/why-unitarian-universalism-is-dying.pdf

Mattis, R. (2022), "Reflection on General Assembly 2022," https://fifthprincipleproject.org/2022/07/12/reflection-on-general-assembly-2022-by-rebecca-mattis/

McWhorter, J. (2020), "Kneeling in the Church of Social Justice," https://reason.com/2020/06/29/kneeling-in-the-church-of-social-justice/

McWhorter, J. (2021), "Words Have Lost Their Common Meaning," https://www.theatlantic.com/ideas/archive/2021/03/nation-divided-language/618461/

Muir, F. (2012), "The end of iChurch," https://www.uuworld.org/articles/end-ichurch

Paul, P. (2022), "She Wrote a Dystopian Novel. What Happened Next Was Pretty Dystopian," https://www.nytimes.com/2022/06/12/opinion/sandra-newman-men.html

Pine, M. (2019), "The UU Crisis Explained," http://www.trulyopenmindsandhearts.blog/2019/10/01/the-uu-crisis-explained

Sickafoose, M. (2019), "Standing on the Side of Power," https://cycleback.files.wordpress.com/2022/03/standing-on-the-side-of-power.pdf

Steele, J. (2006), "White Guilt and the End of the Civil Rights Era," https://www.npr.org/templates/story/story.php?storyId=5385701

Trudeau, R. (2019), "UUMA Board to Ministers: Shut Up!", https://trulyopenmindsandhearts.blog/2019/12/21/uuma-board-to-ministers-shut-up/

Trudeau, R. (2022), "A UU Minister's Warning to a UU Congregation," https://www.youtube.com/watch?v=IGKHfHj8smk

Tweet J (2020), "UU Leadership and Lay People", https://fifthprincipleproject.org/wp-content/uploads/2020/06/UU-Leadership-and-Lay-People.pdf

UU Ministers (2020), "We Quit Letter," uusalem.org/wp-content/uploads/2020/12/We-Quit-UUMA-letter-as-delivered.pdf

UUA (2017), "Why Look a Racism in the UUA?," https://www.uua.org/sites/live-new.uua.org/files/coic_talk_race_uua_112017.pdf

UUA (2018), "Dismantle White Supremacy," https://www.uua.org/justice/dismantle-white-supremacy

UUA (2020), "Widening The Circle of Concern," https://www.uua.org/uuagovernance/committees/cic/widening/theology

UUA (2020), "UUA Membership Statistics, 1961-2020," https://www.uua.org/data/demographics/uua-statistics?

UUA (2021). "Undoing Systemic White Supremacy: A Call to Prophetic Action," https://www.uua.org/action/statements/undoing-systemic-white-supremacy

UUA (2022), "List of Certified Congregations," https://dyn.uua.org/congregation/certlist.php?

UUA BOT (2022), "UUA Board Statement Responding to 2022 Contested Elections," https://www.uua.org/uuagovernance/board/announcements/board-statement-about-2022-contested-elections

UUA NER (2019), "Anti-Racism/Anti-Oppression/Multiculturalism Resources," https://www.uua.org/new-england/resources-tools/anti-racism/anti-oppression/multiculturalism

UUMA (2019), "Announcement of Censure," https://www.facebook.com/uuministers/photos/a.10151038277677757/10155972052887757

UUMUAC (2022), MAC Arrow, https://www.uumuac.org/_files/ugd/51a1b4_d605cb4bad6848d6868d3dbb1c60e327.pdf

VUU (2018), "Intentionality Radical and Spiritual—the VUU #185," https://www.youtube.com/watch?v=VdVzGNb5SmE

Walton, C. (2019), "Mission Priorities," http://uuworld.org/articles/editor-winter-2019

Wells, S. (2019), "The Gadfly Papers," https://www.revscottwells.com/2019/06/23/the-gadfly-papers/

Wells, S. (2019), "The UUMA is dead to me," www.revscottwells.com/2019/08/17/the-uuma-is-dead-to-me/

Westside UU (2021), "Westside Survey Results on UUA," wsuu.org/wp-content/uploads/2021/02/WSUU.UUASurveyResults2.pdf

14 A Jewish Perspective

I joined a UU congregation several years ago because of its welcoming diversity of views and freedom of thought, and its slogan of "We don't have to think alike to love alike." The congregation remains liberal. However, a non-UU friend recently asked me if I ever experienced antisemitism, and I said, "Only in national UU spaces."

Rigid small-mindedness, such as what's coming from the current national UUA and seminaries, is a key source of bigotry. Whether in the left or right, binary "us versus them" thinking and caste systems always result in bigotry and injustice. Eric Hoffer wrote, "Mass movements can rise and spread without belief in a God, but never without belief in a devil."

While this chapter focuses on a Jewish perspective and experience, it could come from within any demographic. I could have as easily written a chapter about how dogmatisms and illiberalism are oppressive of the disabled. I've heard concerns about the current UUA from women, lesbian, gay, and racial and ethnic minority UUs, along with white males.

This chapter has two essays that were published elsewhere in different forms.

The first, titled "How Critical Race Theory Can Be Antisemitic," discusses how a dogmatic application of critical race theory as the only lens to view society is antisemitic.

The second, titled "How Intolerance, Censorship, and Dogmatism Make Unitarian Universalism Increasingly Unwelcome to Jews," explains how Judaism and Jewish culture are about questioning, diversity of views, dissent, and debate—all things traditionally associated with UU—and how any space that is dogmatic and illiberal will be unwelcoming to most Jews.

* * * *

How Critical Race Theory Can Be Antisemitic

"All models are false, but some are useful." —George E.P. Box

It once dawned on me why some people believe antisemitism is a problem within some American and British progressive movements. A—I didn't say *the*, as I know people on the left with different definitions—standard definition amongst many progressives and progressive movements is that **racism = prejudice + power**. As these groups define Jews as part of the white privileged, or "white supremacy" (their term for white America) segment of society, that means that the adherents to that definition are saying antisemitism isn't racism. Or, if they say antisemitism is racism, they've undercut their own definition.

Perhaps they say that antisemitism is not racism but a different form of bigotry, and that is a fair topic for debate. How to define race, what is race, and the question of if Jews are a race are interesting questions.

Many scholars, the United Nations, and the World Jewish Congress define antisemitism as a type of racism, and many textbooks and international laws define racism as including both race and ethnicity. Anne Frank House states that race is an artificial cultural construct and, thus, Jews are not a race, but that the classification of Jews as a race and discrimination based on that is racism.

A Jewish friend said the question of whether Jews are a race or ethnicity is a matter of semantics and joked, "When you find out which we are, let me know." This all says that the world, societies, structures, concepts, and ethnic oppression are far more complex and nuanced than a simplistic equation or definition can encompass.

American racial color categories are artificial and arbitrary, and people on all parts of the political spectrum have long drawn the lines to suit their political ideologies and agendas. Brandy Shufutinsky of the Jewish Institute for Liberal Values said, "I don't use white Jews or Jews of color. A Jew is a Jew is a Jew." She says the prevailing "colorism" is American-centric and that "Jews predate race." (JILV 2021)

There is no denying that the American artificial color code constructs have been socially and psychologically influential in American history and used for ill. Though, as this essay shows, many Jews say artificial color codes and stereotyping that have been decried are now being used by the far left to pigeonhole and oppress them. They point out the hypocrisy and that two wrongs don't make a right.

A problem with power as a required element in the definition is that Jews have been persecuted (as a race—at least that's how the Nazis defined them and how white supremacists define them—and, according to Anne Frank House, that is thus racism) in major part because of the stereotype that they had power. It should disturb that some movements in today's far left use this same trope that has been and is used by antisemitic movements on the far right, including the KKK and Neo-Nazis.

In the 1800s to early 1900s many elite American and Canadian universities, including Harvard, Yale, Columbia, Cornell, McGill, and Toronto, had quotas on Jews in part because they were perceived as being too successful. Physics Nobel Prize winner Richard Feynman could not get into Columbia University as an undergraduate because of quotas on Jews, and National Medal of Science winner Norbert Wiener was rejected for a professorship at Harvard due to a similar quota. Interestingly, Feynman was secular and identified himself as Jewish only ethnically.

The Nazis and white supremacists defined/define Jews as both having power/privilege and being an inferior people/race. This all points out that there are many ways, types, and directions of discrimination, racism, oppression, and persecution.

Another common point that is brought up is that it is incorrect, or at the very least problematic, to generalize across all members about their privilege and power. There have been many poor and powerless Jews and Jewish communities throughout history, and a homeless opioid-addicted white man in rural West Virginia will likely question the existence of his privilege and power in the United States.

Rabbi Michael Lerner, of Beyt Tikkun Synagogue in Berkeley, says the privileged categorization is a stereotype. "This argument leaves out the hundreds of thousands of Jews who have not 'made it' the way their Manhattan brothers and sisters may have." A Jewish friend, whose grandparents were poor immigrants from Eastern Europe, chafes at the privileged generalization. He says, "We have been listening to this white privilege stuff for 5,000 years." (Lerner 2019)

A complaint from many Jews is that some movements and people within the far left trivialize or dismiss the significance of antisemitism, and many Jews say that some progressive movements are antisemitic. That has been an accusation of British Labour and the BDS (Boycott, Divest, and Sanction) movement. (Playto 2019)

History professor KC Johnson said, "If Jews are seen as 'white' (which, in this permutation of progressivism, they are), and 'whites' cannot be subjected to racist attacks, then antisemitism becomes a trivial concern." (Johnson in Dunst 2018)

The 2019 LGBT+ DC Dyke March organizers banned marchers from carrying the Israeli flag (other flags were allowed) and banners with the Star of David symbol. A Jewish friend said, "Say hello to the new boss, same as the old boss." A gay Israeli Jew who considers the Israeli flag "the Jewish Pride flag" wrote that the "ban says I should be ashamed of my nationality and my faith rather than be accepted for who I am." (Mazzig 2019)

I was talking with an English Jewess in London. As an American curious about her perspective, I asked her if she thought there was antisemitism in the British Labour Party, and she said, "Yes, in my opinion, and generally in the left." I said, "Some within the American extreme left use the same stereotypes about Jews as the far right." Her response was, "Yes, exactly."

In recent years, there have been Jewish criticism and even protests of Unitarian Universalist congregations and UU over concerns of antisemitism embedded in the UUA's increasingly extremist political ideology. This has been due to the widespread showing of what many Jews considered an antisemitic documentary, neo-racist and one-sided theories and language about Jews and Israel, censorship, and the adoption of divisive political positions. (McArdle 2016) (Stevens 2017) (Leblang 2017) (UUCS 2019)

Robert Walker, director of Hasbara Fellowships Canada, says that radical left activists on university campuses often dismiss the opinions of Jews, including on issues of discrimination, because Jews are catalogued as privileged (Lungen 2018).

Walker says: "Our fellows have seen more instances where a pro-Israel side is dismissed in a summary manner, merely because many of our students are Jews, (and are) therefore seen to be privileged and therefore excluded from consideration or mainstream dialogue. . . . Their opinion is often dismissed for being Jewish or pro-Israel and seen as part of the privileged white bourgeoisie. . . . People are dismissed simply for who they are. We're seeing this more and more." (Walker in Lungen 2018)

Rabbi Lerner says many Jews, including he, do not consider Jews white and he considers categorizing Jews as white as an act of oppression. He says some on the far left categorize Jews as white as an attempt to paint them not as historically marginalized and persecuted people with their own unique culture and history, but as a part of the generic oppressive power structure. Lerner writes, "Jews are not white, and those who claim we are and exclude our history and literature from their newly emerging multicultural canon are our oppressors. . . . Jews can only be deemed 'white' if there is massive amnesia on the part of non-Jews about the monumental history of anti-Semitism." (Lerner 2019)

In the *Times of Israel* essay "Are Jews a People of Color?," Dani Ishai Behan writes, "All throughout history, the racial othering of Jews has led to some pretty horrific results, so it is understandable why some would prefer to leave race/ethnicity out of the equation altogether. But at the same time, conceptualizing Jews as either 'white' or 'just a religion,' as many of our detractors are wont to do, helps to perpetuate a culture of antisemitism on the antiracist left. That is to say, if we are 'just white people with funny hats,' then we are perforce not 'really' an oppressed group, thereby enabling antiracists to retain their credentials without having to listen to Jews or take our concerns seriously." (Behan 2017)

Pamela Paresky, of the University of Chicago's Stevanovich Institute, writes, "In the critical social justice paradigm, Jews, who have never been seen as white by those for whom being white is a moral good, are now seen as white by those for whom whiteness is an unmitigated evil." (Paresky 2019)

I attended a Unitarian Universalist racial justice meeting where a zealous supporter of critical race theory did not want the group to read an article by a Jewish professor "because he is white." She wanted a vetter to prevent articles from such voices from even reaching group members. I am not generalizing about the group, as two group members said they thought the article was worthy of discussion, if in a different forum.

Whatever one's definitions of the terms, the rhetorical odiousness of telling Auschwitz survivors in Pittsburgh or Charleston that they are part of "white supremacy" and part of the "racist oppression" should be obvious. Following that up by then telling those survivors that any offense they take is "white fragility" is nothing short of gaslighting.

A Jewish woman who objected to being called a member of the "white supremacy" by people on the far left explained, "It is not a matter of intellectually debating the issue. It simply is offensive."

I know people on the left, progressives, racial minorities, and Jews with a wide variety of opinions and views and considerations, including on this topic. I am not painting with a broad brush or generalizing. I know many progressives and racial minorities do not subscribe to that definition of racism and its antiracism theory.

However, as with any theory or model, a key is how the "racism = prejudice + power" definition is considered.

The recently deceased Physics Nobel Prize winner and philosopher of science Phillip Anderson was an antireductionist and was for complexity in modeling. He correctly saw that reality, and any area within it, was far too complex and nuanced to be reduced to a simple theory or model, and said that "more is different." (Horgan 2020)

All models and theories are artificial and, thus, false representations of reality. However, when used and considered as one of many different lenses through which to view things, a theory can be useful and offer insight. Science uses multiple and often competing theories to examine an area, each theory limited but together giving a fuller, if still incomplete, picture. Philosopher Paul Feyerabend correctly wrote, "No theory ever agrees with all the facts in its domain."

The antiracism "racism = prejudice + power" definition and theory is an interesting and useful lens to view things through. However, as with any theory, it is too simplistic and must be just one of many different lenses through which to look at the complexity of racism, oppression, and society. Making it the only lens—and making it dogma and ideology, and saying that no other lenses, theories, or viewpoints can be expressed or used—is false and foolish.

Race, racism, ethnicity, oppression, marginalization, and bigotry are incredibly complex and multifaceted areas, full of gray areas, diversity, contradictions, paradoxes, subjectivity, and diverse personal life experiences that cannot be defined, much less solved, by one model, theory, or equation. Jews demonstrate that one can both be privileged and marginalized, that oppression and persecution can involve both punching down and punching up, and that someone can both be oppressed and an oppressor.

Author of *How to Fight Anti-Semitism* Bari Weiss said that there is "good anti-racism and bad anti-racism," and that the bad kind—one, she writes, that "has dangerous implications for Jews"—is the current neo-racist version pushed by authors such as Robin DiAngelo and Ibram X. Kendi. Weiss says that good antiracism "reflects the idea that we should be judged by the content of our character and not the color of our skin, the kind of anti-racism that insists on our common humanity, the kind of anti-racism that no one should be inheritors of collective guilt or inheritors of collective innocence, that we should all be judged as individuals." (Weiss 2020)

If the "racism = prejudice + power" definition and critical race theory are dogmatically used as the sole or key definition and lens through which to view the world, social structures, and people—as some and some groups on the far left do—it is clearly antisemitic, using dangerous and ignorant stereotypes, characterizations, and theories about Jews.

The irony is, as antisemitism where Jews are defined as a racial category is a form of racism, that makes that particular antiracism model racist.

* * * *

How Intolerance, Censorship and Dogmatism Make Unitarian Universalism Increasingly Unwelcoming to Jews

"Debate is a sacred Jewish sacrament." —Rabbi David Wolpe

"When I came home from school my mother would never ask me, 'What did you learn today?' Only, 'Did you ask a good question?'" —Physics Nobel Prize-winner Isidor Rabi

Judaism is a traditional part of Unitarian Universalism. Judaism is unitarian, and UU lists Jewish teachings as one of its sources. Michael Servetus hoped that, in its contrast to the prevailing Trinitarianism, Unitarianism would attract Jews and Muslims.

Jewish belief is about the interdependent web of life, stewardship and repair of the earth, living ethically, and being concerned about life on Earth rather than some speculative afterlife. It is about personal spiritual paths and personal definitions of God, not to mention the inclusion of Jews who are secular, atheist, and agnostic. Most would catalog me as agnostic.

It all sounds an awful lot like UU, doesn't it? A Jewish friend said, "In theory, UUism is very much in the spirit of Judaism: ministers as teachers, not priests, congregational polity, and all that."

I'm a Maskil, a Jewish title given to me by an interfaith rabbi and Hebrew for "scholar." Historically, the maskilim were followers of the Haskalah or Jewish Enlightenment. The Haskalah promoted rationalism, liberalism, freedom of thought and inquiry, and the promotion of secular education, art, and sciences in Jewish culture and schools. It is the genesis of today's Reform, Progressive, Liberal and secular Judaism. Again, it may remind some of UU.

You can imagine what I and many UUs think when the radical ideologues in the UUA and UUMA demean logic, liberalism, the Enlightenment, and freedom of thought and inquiry.

The importance of debate, questioning, and dissent in Judaism

Judaism is about the diversity of viewpoints, debate, questioning, and dissent.

Debate has been an essential part of Judaism since its formation, and this is reflected throughout the Torah. Israel is Hebrew for "Wrestling (debating/arguing) with God." Moses, Jacob and Abraham argued with God, with Moses winning the debate and changing God's mind! The Hebrew Bible says, "God loves it when you argue with him." One of the key Jewish theologians and philosophers of the twentieth century, Abraham Joshua Hershel, wrote, "Dissent is indigenous to Judaism." Catholics and fundamentalist Christians often find Judaism disconcerting because Jews are not taught to intellectually submit to a fundamentalist orthodoxy, the Torah, or God.

Rabbis teach the laity, including children, that questioning is the path to deeper understanding. A tradition of Passover is that the children get to ask the adults questions and the adults have to answer sincerely. Chancellor Emeritus of the Jewish Theological Seminary Ismar Schorsch writes, "The Seder both celebrates and circumscribes the right to question. Our children are invited to participate to the hilt by showering us with whatever questions might be on their minds. Judaism does not take refuge in dogmatism." (Schorsch 2000)

I've half-joked to my UU friends that "Judaism is more UU than UU."

However, I have witnessed UU at the national, organizational and seminary levels moving away from religious liberalism. I have seen trends toward top-down orthodoxy, groupthink, and expectations of ideological and political conformity. I have seen shaming and shunning of people who express different viewpoints that fall well within the parameters of UU's Principles.

It should go without saying that a dogmatic UUA and ministers that suppress debate and heterodoxy make UU inhospitable to many Jews and Jewish culture.

A Jewish friend resigned from his UU congregation last year due to dogmatism and groupthink. I said, "Being Jewish means asking questions and debating different viewpoints. Not allowing questioning or debating would make Unitarian Universalism inhospitable to Jews." He replied: "And—dare I say it?—antisemitic."

Jewish criticism of extreme left social justice ideologies

There has been much Jewish concern over the neo-racist ideology, radical political positions, and stifling of debate in many quarters as advocated by the UUA. These include from prominent Jewish thinkers such as Pamela Paresky, Steven Pinker, Jonathan Haidt, KC Johnson, Eliot Cohen, and Jerry Coyne, and the Jewish Institute for Liberal Values. Agree or disagree with them, they are Jewish voices that should be heard in UU. I can assure you that there are Jews in UU congregations who agree with many of these views. (JILV 2021)

Jews, including within Reform and Progressive Judaism and within UU, have a wide diversity of views, and some Jews agree with the UUA dogma. I am not suggesting otherwise. Though a small minority, there are Jews who are anti-Zionist. I have a Jewish professor friend who supports critical race theory, and we enjoy debating these issues with each other.

The issue is that with the diversity of views and most Jews disagreeing with UUA-style dogma and intolerance, a UUA and ministers that expect adherence to one narrow ideology or political stance, or that say that "only Jews who agree with our dogma are truly welcome and listened to," make UU inhospitable to many Jews.

Another Jewish friend who recently quit UU told me that he was scared to speak his views in UU forums due to the atmosphere of intolerance to different views.

Last year I had a newly ordained true believer minister tell me she felt that I did not belong in UU for having and expressing what are perfectly mainstream Jewish views that fall well within the parameters of UU's Principles. When I relayed what she said to a longtime minister, he replied, "She should re-read UU's principles."

When I posted both essays in this chapter in a UU forum, a UUA-aligned minister said that these essays were "racist dog whistles" and "alt-right" (standard ad hominem attacks these days to any dissent by UUs) and compared me and these essays to Alex Jones. Another minister told others to ignore what I wrote because I was "white" (ironic, as the minister was white).

Yet another UUA-aligned true believer responded only by asking what I thought about "Palestinian babies in cages."

I was shocked by their complete ignorance and closed-mindedness, but even more that it came from young UU ministers. They came across as indoctrinated political zealots, and I did not understand how such small-minded people were qualified to be UU ministers. They likely held themselves up as socialist justice activists.

I then remembered that I had seen similar ad hominem attacks by new ministers and national leaders on others who dared dissent. For dogmatists who believe their narrow view is the only truth, anyone with a different viewpoint is the enemy.

This essay isn't just about Jews and Jews in UU, but about how general UUA trends of intolerance, dogma, and censorship are oppressive of all groups, minority and majority. I know that this bigotry I experienced was born out of ignorance and people indoctrinated to see things only in binary ways. In a self-righteous movement that categorizes the expression of any divergent thought as "harmful," "racist," and "oppression" and dissenters as the enemy, their small-minded ire would have been applied to anyone who dissented.

I had published a different version of this essay elsewhere, and a comment in the comment section was: "How Intolerance, Censorship and Dogmatism Make Unitarian Universalism Increasingly Unwelcoming to Jews . . . and All Thinking People."

References

Arzoumanian, A. (2020), "Armenians and Race: A Personal Response to an Impossible Question," thecolgatemaroonnews.com/23987/commentary/armenians-and-race-a-personal-response-to-an-impossible-question/

Behan, D (2017), "Are Jews a People of Color?", https://blogs.timesofisrael.com/are-jews-a-people-of-color/

Dunst, C. (2018), "Is antisemitism a form of racism?", .jpost.com/Diaspora/Antisemitism/Is-antisemitism-a-form-of-racism-564712

Flayton, B. (2019), "On the Frontlines of Progressive Anti-Semitism," nytimes.com/2019/11/14/opinion/college-israel-anti-semitism.html

Goldman, S. (2021), "What We Lose When We Lose Thomas Jefferson," bariweiss.substack.com/p/what-we-lose-when-we-lose-thomas

Horgan, J. (2020), "Philip Anderson, Gruff Guru of Physics and Complexity Research, Dies," blogs.scientificamerican.com/cross-check/philip-anderson-gruff-guru-of-physics-and-complexity-research-dies/

JILV, "New Paradigms in Black-Jewish Relations," youtube.com/watch?v=FoMxV0Szb7M

JILV (2021), "Letter to fellow Jews on equality and liberal values," https://jilv.org/be-heard/

Leblang, D. "Area Jews ask: Why would a church show an anti-Semitic movie?", jewishjournal.org/2017/11/02/area-jews-ask-why-would-a-church-show-an-anti-semitic-movie/

Lerner, M. (2019), "Jews Are Not White," villagevoice.com/2019/07/25/the-white-issue-jews-are-not-white/

Lungen, P. (2018), "Check Your Jewish Privilege," cjnews.com/living-jewish/check-your-jewish-privilege

Mazzig, H. (2019), "The D.C. Dyke March barred the Jewish pride flag. This LGBTQ space no longer feels safe," https://www.nbcnews.com/think/opinion/d-c-dyke-march-barred-jewish-pride-flag-lgbtq-space-ncna1015786

McArdle, E. (2016), "Rabbi Jacobs: Why I raised divestment concerns during celebration," uuworld.org/articles/uuaga2016jacobsdivestment

Paresky, P. (2019), "Critical Race Theory and the 'Hyper White Jew'", sapirjournal.org/social-justice/2021/05/critical-race-theory-and-the-hyper-white-jew/

Schorch I (2020), "The Right to Question," https://www.jtsa.edu/torah/the-right-to-question/

Stevens, C. (2017), "Dispute erupts over film on Israel at Unitarian Universalist Church of Marblehead," marblehead.wickedlocal.com/news/20171031/dispute-erupts-over-film-on-israel-at-unitarian-universalist-church-of-marblehead

UUCS (2019), "Todd's Thoughts May 2019," uuspokane.org/WP2/2019/04/25/todds-thoughts-may-2019/

Weiss, B. (2021), "Stop Being Shocked: American liberalism is in danger from a new ideology—one with dangerous implications for Jews," tabletmag.com/sections/news/articles/stop-being-shocked

15 Why the UUA Is Probably Doomed to Fail in Its Goals

The current national UU leadership has expressed that it aspires to both increase UU membership and greatly increase racial minority membership by moving an already politically left UU even further to left into radicalism. These goals can conflict, and the current national UU's attempts may produce neither.

It's not just racial minorities: UU culture is unwelcoming to the majority in most demographics

Usually omitted in the argument that UU culture excludes most racial minorities—and in the mind of some is thus "racist"—is the fact that UU is unwelcoming to most whites. Many outsiders would describe the current UU as a counterculture. That it does not appeal to the large majority of all demographics is why it's tiny. My white libertarian friend from Texas would follow the UU's Principles and is a fan of the Unitarian psychologist Julian Jaynes. He told me he could stand about ten seconds of UU's brand of identity politics, politically correctness, and "Christian lite" services.

I have talked to atheists who I thought might be attracted to a church that has atheists and shares their political persuasion. The majority of the small sample had no interest in joining a UU congregation because they don't want to belong to any organized church, even one that has atheists and agnostics, and attend services that have a church-like style.

Many working-class and working-class background UUs have long complained about classicism in UU and UU congregations. This remains. Most proponents of the prevailing UUA-style social justice and identity politics are university-educated cultural elites who are often out of touch with and even dismissive of working-class and poor American cultures and views. (Loury 2022)

A complaint about the recent years' narrowing of UU's politics is that it excludes political moderates and conservatives who would embrace the UU Principles. There is no political litmus test to be a UU, and there is no reason that many moderates, libertarians, and conservatives who believe in "the inherent worth and dignity of every person" can't belong to a UU or other religiously liberal church. As UU Minister Rev. Sean Neil-Baron put it, "We are a liberal religion, not a religion for liberals," and there used to be an active group for conservative UUs. (UUA 2017) (Morgenstern 2020)

I know UUs who have said they wish their congregational membership had a broader political spectrum. Many UUs are rotely dismissive and even openly disdainful of conservatives, wrongly assuming all UU congregants have progressive views.

In a poll of a Seattle area congregation, all those who said the congregation was unwelcoming to visitors were white. While my congregation has a greeters team that welcomes and assists all who enter the doors, I've heard from others that some congregations can be aloof and cliquish. I suspect that some racial and ethnic minorities incorrectly interpret this general aloofness as personal slight.

Moving further left makes UU only more unappealing to most minorities

About fourteen percent of the country is black. It is simply the statistical reality that if every church wants to be, say, forty percent black, that is impossible. UU, in its traditional or current state, will not be the type of church that attracts large swaths of blacks and other racial and ethnic minorities.

In her 2017 essay "Where Are We Headed?", UU minister Rev. Kate Braestrup wrote that UU would have to become more conservative and welcoming to a broader range of political views to attract many minorities, who are generally more conservative than UU. (Braestrup 2017)

As earlier documented, large majorities of all racial and ethnic groups reject UUA-style politically correct culture and language. Further, Pew Research Center polling has shown that the far left ("progressive left") is only 6% of the United States population and is predominantly non-Hispanic white and culturally elite (highly educated and economically privileged). Similarly, a 2021 national education poll reported that the "extreme woke" (dismantle society, students should be taught that whites are oppressors and non-whites are oppressed, etc.) make up 6% of the population and is disproportionally non-Hispanic white and culturally/socially elite. (Pew Research Center 2021) (Sumner 2022)

According to a 2020 Pew Research Center Poll, 65 percent of black Democrats identify as moderate or conservative, and only 37 percent of Hispanic Democrats identify as progressives. By a wide margin, whites are the most likely to be in the far left of the Democratic Party. (Pew Research Center 2021) (Pew Research Center 2020) (Winston 2020)

In short, the far left and extreme woke is a tiny, culturally elite and predominantly white group that does not represent the views or desires of most minorities. An Indian man told me he left his UU congregation because he no longer felt welcome due to his more conservative views.

Taking various fringe political positions unpopular with most minorities, the UUA has called for the abolishment of police and for congregations to quit calling the police. A 2021 national poll showed that only 23 percent of blacks, 16 percent of Hispanics and 22 percent of Asians support reducing spending on police. Polls over the years have consistently shown that the large majority of all racial and ethnic groups want the same or more spending on police and the same or larger police presence in their neighborhoods. (UUA 2020) (Pew Research Center 2021) (Gallup 2020) (Parker & Hurst 2021) (Hirsi 2021)

Civil rights leader and Democratic Party Whip James Clyburn said that the "Defund the Police" sloganeering cost Democrats seats in the 2020 election and harmed the Black Lives Matter cause. Congressional Black Caucus Chair Rep. Karen Bass called Defund the Police "probably one of the worst slogans ever." (Brown 2020) (Moore 2020)

The national UU and UU groups have aligned themselves with extremist Jewish groups and movements that are out of step with majority Jewish views and even labeled as antisemitic by mainstream Jewish organizations. (McCardle 2016) (Leblang 2017) (ADL 2015)

A white-dominant church or congregation will not attract most racial and ethnic minorities by adopting unpopular and sometimes even offending language and political positions.

Rev. Braestrup wrote: "Despite our decades of self-flagellating attempts to scour away every vestige of racism from our bleeding hearts, religions that have never made the slightest effort to 'dismantle white supremacy' aren't just more successful at attracting congregants of all colors, they are—according to our own preferred measures—far less racist. . . . The statistics, in other words, strongly imply that anyone who wishes to belong to a non-racist church should depart Unitarian Universalism and join the Assemblies of God. Or—easier still—become a Catholic." (Braestrup 2017)

While UUs like to think of themselves as independent thinkers and open-minded, I find them to be as much group thinkers and crowd followers as in any religious denomination. UU spaces are often political and ideological bubbles, unaware of or dismissing different viewpoints including those from minorities. A UU said that to many UUs multiculturalism means, "People who think like us but come in different colors." I replied, "Multiculturalism means they aren't all going to think like you, and many will think things you very much disagree with."

Former UU Sasha Kwapinski wrote, "They talk a lot about tolerance and diversity—until you disagree with them."

UU leaders often hold up the goals of multiculturalism and diversity. However, they don't really want multiculturalism and diversity. A multicultural and diverse church would contain diverse political, social, and ideological ideas and values. With their new expectations of political and ideological conformity, national UU leaders are trying to create a monoculture that ironically excludes most minorities.

Conflicting Goals

The UUA's efforts are not just about attracting minorities to UU but about being more inclusive and empowering of the minorities already in UU. The latter is important but causes a conflict.

Racial minorities in UU tend to be much further to the political left, more radical and identity-politics-centric than the general racial minority population. UU these days advertises itself as a safe space, so it attracts from a very small percentage within minority groups that feel they need emotional safe spaces.

Many white UUs and white progressives are under the mistaken impression that radical minority activists are proxies for their entire demographics. This often is because UU leaders and ideologues falsely say that these fringe views are the majority views and the only "authentic" voice of minorities. UUs are learning about race issues and race relations from a tiny group that is unrepresentative of the larger minority groups.

Doing what "BIPOC of UU ask us to do" will make UU even less appealing to most outside racial minorities. The radicalization of UU may not only fail to attract many racial minorities to UU but will lead to many religious liberals leaving. (Hirsi 2021)

The conflict is exemplified by the word Latinx. UU works to be LGBT+ inclusive and the UUA, *UU World*, and many UU congregations and groups commonly use the term Latinx. Latinx is seen as gender-inclusive but is off-putting to most Latinos. (Douthat 2019)

The use of "Latinx" demonstrates that UU aspires for the diversity and inclusion of numerous minority identities, not just racial and ethnic. In both practice and theory, this is a conundrum because minority cultures and demographics are never in exact alignment with each other. That's why it's a challenge to create successful multi-cultural and interfaith organizations. People with multiple identities often experience such internal conflicts.

It is problematic when UUs want ethnic and racial minorities to be part of their church but only if they "think the way we do." I see a tokenizing and fetishism in focusing strictly on the percentage of skin colors in a congregation, and a pandering in doing whatever it takes to attract people of different skin colors. There always has been an arrogant strain of far left white activists who condescendingly feel that they know what is right for minorities.

I wonder about UU laity who are so easily and sometimes unquestioningly willing to discard their long-held UU values such as religious liberalism, self-determination, due process, diversity of individual views and paths, and freedom of expression and speech simply because a group of self-anointed authorities in classes and the pulpit instruct them to. It makes me wonder what other values they'd be willing to throw overboard in the name of a cause, because of the color of someone's skin or to go along with a crowd.

UU Minister Rev. Craig Moro wrote, "I suspect one of the things that drives 'BIPOC' folks away after a visit or two is that some UUs seem to be trying to 'collect' them—to add them to some sort of collection of skins and heads. That would scare me, too!"

An Asian man who quit UU wrote, "The tone of the entire organization has shifted more and more left and privileged as time goes on. . . . When a person of color does show up (myself included), it was ridiculous. Our opinions were not valued because they were our opinions, but simply because of the color of our skin. In trying to be more inclusive, the organization became more racist. No non-white person wants to get in a room and watch rich white people flog themselves all day and apologize for transgressions that may or may not have ever happened. It is tiresome and has nothing to do with fellowship. It just makes those members feel better."

I believe the UUA's attempt to move UU further to the left into extremism, both generally but in particular in the area of identity politics, and to try to create ideological and political homogony will neither attract substantial numbers of racial and ethnic minorities nor expand UU membership. My prediction is that UU membership will fall even more drastically. In fact, it was soon after I wrote this chapter the UUA published the most dramatic drop in membership and congregations in church history.

References

8th Principle (2021), "Where Did This Come From Originally?", https://www.8thprincipleuu.org/background

ADL (2015), "BDS: The Global Campaign to Delegitimize Israel," https://www.adl.org/resources/backgrounders/bds-the-global-campaign-to-delegitimize-israel

Brown, M. (2020), "Democratic Whip James Clyburn: 'Defund the police' cost Democrats seats, hurt Black Lives Matter movement," https://www.usatoday.com/story/news/politics/2020/11/08/james-clyburn-defund-police-cost-democrats-seats-hurt-black-lives-matter/6216371002/

Blake, J. (2010), "Why Sunday morning remains America's most segregated hour," https://religion.blogs.cnn.com/2010/10/06/why-sunday-morning-remains-americas-most-segregated-hour/

Braestrup, K. (2017), "Where Are We Headed?", https://trulyopenmindsandhearts.blog/2017/11/21/where-are-we-headed/

CLFUU (2017), "Intentionally Radical AND Spiritual—The VUU," https://www.youtube.com/watch?v=VdVzGNb5SmE

Coyne, J. (2022), "The annual evolution meeting raises some questions," https://whyevolutionistrue.com/2022/05/12/the-annual-evolution-meeting-raises-some-questions/

Cunningham, V. (2017), "The Case for Black English," https://www.newyorker.com/magazine/2017/05/15/the-case-for-black-english

Douthat, R. (2019), "Democrats' Latinx Problem," https://www.nytimes.com/2019/11/05/opinion/latinix-warren-democrats.html

Frederick-Gray, S. (2021), "Sea Change, Not Slow Change," https://www.uuworld.org/articles/president-fall-2021

Gallup (2020), "Black Americans Want Police to Retain Local Presence," https://news.gallup.com/poll/316571/black-americans-police-retain-local-presence.aspx

Grossman, C. (2015), "Sunday Is Still the Most Segregated Day of the Week," https://www.americamagazine.org/content/all-things/sunday-still-most-segregated-day-week

Halsted, J. (2019), "My Church Is Dying and I'm OK with That," https://praywithyourfeet.org/2019/12/17/my-church-is-dying-and-im-ok-with-that/

Hirsi, I. (2021), "Black Residents of Minneapolis Say They Need More Cops—Not Fewer," https://www.thenation.com/article/politics/minneapolis-police-reform/

Leblang, D. (2017), "Area Jews ask: Why would a church show an anti-Semitic movie?", https://www.jewishjournal.org/2017/11/02/area-jews-ask-why-would-a-church-show-an-anti-semitic-movie/

Loehr, D. (2005), "Why Unitarian Universalism is Dying," https://files.meadville.edu/files/resources/why-unitarian-universalism-is-dying.pdf

Loury, G. (2022), "Why Does Racial Inequality Persist?", https://glennloury.substack.com/p/why-does-racial-inequality-persist?s=r

Manhattan Institute (2021) "Critical Race Theory: On the New Ideology of Race," https://www.youtube.com/watch?v=ZuvhrXM3v7U&t=4495s

McArdle, E. (2016), "Rabbi Jacobs: Why I raised divestment concerns during celebration," http://uuworld.org/articles/uuaga2016jacobsdivestment

McCardle, E. (2017), "Two-thirds of UU congregations participate in White Supremacy Teach-In," https://www.uuworld.org/articles/two-thirds-participate-teach

McWhorter, J. (2022), "BIPOC is Jargon. That's OK, and Normal People Don't Have to Use It," https://www.nytimes.com/2022/03/25/opinion/bipoc-latinx.html

Monk, Y. (2018), "Americans Strongly Dislike PC Culture," http://theatlantic.com/ideas/archive/2018/10/large-majorities-dislike-political-correctness/572581/

Moore M (2020), "Congressional Black Caucus chair: 'Defund the police' is 'one of the worst slogans ever'", https://nypost.com/2020/06/16/black-caucus-chair-defund-the-police-is-one-of-the-worst-slogans/

Morgenstern, A. (2020), "Conservative Values for Unitarian Universalists," https://www.uucpa.org/services/conservative-values-for-unitarian-universalists-2/

Parker & Hurst (2021), "Growing share of Americans say they want more spending on police in their area," https://www.pewresearch.org/fact-tank/2021/10/26/growing-share-of-americans-say-they-want-more-spending-on-police-in-their-area/

Pew Research Center (2015), "The most and least racially diverse U.S. religious groups," https://www.pewresearch.org/fact-tank/2015/07/27/the-most-and-least-racially-diverse-u-s-religious-groups/

Pew Research Center (2020), "5 facts about black Democrats," https://www.pewresearch.org/fact-tank/2020/02/27/5-facts-about-black-democrats/

Pew Research Center (2021) "Facts About the U.S. Black Population," https://www.pewresearch.org/social-trends/fact-sheet/facts-about-the-us-black-population/

Pew Research Center (2021), "Progressive Left", https://www.pewresearch.org/politics/2021/11/09/progressive-left/

Pew Research Center (2021), "Growing share of Americans say they want more spending on police in their area", https://www.pewresearch.org/fact-tank/2021/10/26/growing-share-of-americans-say-they-want-more-spending-on-police-in-their-area/

Sumner S (2022), "6 percent of Americans are woke extremists", https://www.econlib.org/6-of-americans-are-woke-extremists/

ThinkNow (2019), "Progressive Latino pollster: 98% of Latinos do not identify with 'Latinx' label," http://medium.com/@ThinkNowTweets/progressive-latino-pollster-trust-me-latinos-do-not-identify-with-latinx-63229adebcea

UUA (1997), "Toward an Anti-Racist Unitarian Universalist Association: 1997 Business Resolution," https://www.uua.org/action/statements/toward-anti-racist-unitarian-universalist-association

UUA (2017), "Conservative Forum for Unitarian Universalists," https://www.uua.org/offices/organizations/conservative-forum-unitarian-universalists

UUA (2020), "UUA Membership Statistics, 1961-2020," https://www.uua.org/data/demographics/uua-statistics

UUA (2020), "The Unitarian Universalist Association Says It's Time to Defund the Police," https://www.uua.org/pressroom/press-releases/unitarian-universalist-association-says-its-time-defund-police

UU World (2010), "Racial and ethnic diversity of Unitarian Universalists," https://www.uuworld.org/articles/racial-ethnic-diversity-uus

Winston, D. (2020), "As Democrats go hard left, Hispanics head to the center," https://rollcall.com/2021/06/23/as-democrats-go-hard-left-hispanics-head-to-the-center/

WSUU (2018), "Beloved Congregations," https://wsuu.org/2018/11/07/sign-up-for-beloved-conversations-groups/

16 Conclusion

There is no one or objectively correct way to tackle issues of racial, ethnic, and other oppression and inequalities. Any model is at best limited, imperfect, and situational and involves trade-offs. While a variety of approaches can be useful, I know that authoritarianism, dogmatism, and illiberalism are not among them. Authoritarianism, dogmatism, and illiberalism are oppressive, including of minorities.

We all have our theories, personal ideologies, and subjective ways of looking at the world. Philosopher Thomas Kuhn wrote, "People see the world through their theories." The problem is when people try to force everyone to adhere to a theory. People and groups who think they've discovered "the one true universal truth" and "the one correct way of viewing the world" and that everyone must follow it are tragic stories as old as humankind. Sadly, as it's an innate trait in human psychology, such fanaticism is found within every new generation.

This text argues for liberalism, the open exchange of ideas, and freedom of speech and expression. (I'm not an absolutist, so no slippery slope arguments.) It argues for the importance of listening to and learning from others' perspectives and ideas to expand our knowledge and understanding. These are essential for democracy, a collective search for truth, and healthy societies, communities, and personal relationships.

Having and maintaining liberal, tolerant communities and institutions that support the respectful exchange of ideas are not passive activities. Illiberalism and censorship don't always come in the form of edicts or rules from authority. They can come via groupthink and crowd following, peer pressure and going along to get along. Self-censorship is censorship. They can come from a culture that doesn't actively foster freedom of expression and dialogue. Thomas Sowell wrote, "Freedom is unlikely to be lost all at once and openly. It is far more likely to be eroded away, bit by bit, amid glittering promises and expressions of noble ideals."

Learn, practice, and promote critical thinking skills.

Appendix

The appendix includes two referenced essays reprinted with permission of the authors, Munro Sickafoose and Jim Aikin.

Appendix 1.1: "Standing on the Side of Power" by UU Minister Rev. Munro Sickafoose

This essay expresses two main contentions. First, that Unitarian Universalism has been misguided into adopting what can only be called a fundamentalist stance by a small group of religious reactionaries, and that this not only damages our faith, but our broader social justice efforts in our communities. The second contention is that they have done so through the misuse and abuse of power of governance, and by undermining our polity and the tenets of our faith through theological and ideological error.

This has been done without any real consent or understanding by our congregations of these changes, and without the necessary debate that should accompany such a radical shift.

ARAOMC as Fundamentalism

I first encountered the doctrine and dogma of ARAOMC (Anti-Racism, Anti-Oppression, Multiculturalism) at Starr King School for the Ministry (SKSM). I entered as an M.Div. student in the Fall of 2008 as a distance learner, and took remote classes in whatever interested me. I had some very cool and open-minded teachers. In 2010, I moved to Berkeley so that I could acquire the necessary residence hours for my degree.

The pedagogy of Starr King at that time was focused on ECO – Educating to Counter Oppressions. The framework was/is ARAOMC. Anti-Racism/Anti-Oppression/Multi-Culturalism, a political ideology cobbled together from a number of sources: CRT, the writings of a number of very brilliant people, the concept of intersectionality, and the opposition to mainstream cultural norms, including whiteness, the patriarchy, gender norms, etc.

Now, I agree that many cultural norms are messed up and damage many lives in any number of ways, and that they need to change. I also agree that the legacy of slavery in the USA is painful and harmful, and that this needs to be addressed. As does the even worse genocide of indigenous peoples. As does the laying waste to the environment we are all guilty of. The lists of fucked upped things are plenty long, and justice and compassion call us to try and rectify the harm that has been done, and is still being done.

This essay isn't about my disagreement with any of those goals.

It's about what I see as the merging of an extreme political ideology into Unitarian Universalism, and its transformation into a reactionary religious movement that exhibits all the hallmarks of fundamentalism.

Characteristics of fundamentalism include – in no particular order of importance:

- Strict adherence to a text or dogma that cannot be questioned
- The existence of an Elect to which the truth is given
- The division of people into those who "get it" and those who don't (woke/unwoke, saved/damned, enlightened/unenlightened, etc., pick your poison.)
- The suppression and excommunication of dissenting voices
- The use of fear, guilt, shaming, scapegoating, gaslighting, etc. as a means of conversion and maintaining power over, rather than power with

- The demonization of some entity, group, or invoking of some abstract force as the reason for the world's evils. (examples: The Devil, the Serbs, the Jews, capitalism, communism, immigrants, white supremacy culture, and so on ad nauseum.)

There are more, but I think that covers the basics.

I contend that joining woke progressive activism with a particular interpretation of Universalist theology has resulted in a reactionary religious fundamentalism that is more interested in ideological purity and power than actual inclusiveness, and that is alienating and ostracizing when we most need solidarity.

This fundamentalism has rejected our Unitarian heritage, and badly damaged our Universalist heritage as well. It is elitist, highly partisan, and political, not religious. It mirrors the ancient alliance of church and state, of politics and religion. It makes the same mistake progressives have accused the religious right of making. It also partakes heavily of ideas from the Counter-Enlightenment-- against rationalism, universalism and empiricism, which are commonly associated with the Enlightenment. It also uses the goals and tactics of the Counter-Reformation.

It is reactionary because it seeks a return to the days when our Puritan ancestors demanded – and got – strict adherence from its members, and governance was hierarchical, by the Elect. It seeks to impose a ideological viewpoint on our congregations and the larger culture.

It is not Unitarian Universalism as we have known it, nor is it an "evolution" of our faith.

A Culture of the Abuse of Power

This essay is also about what I believe is the flawed understanding of power at the heart of ARAOMC thinking, and the misuse and abuses of power by its adherents. Some of that misuse and abuse is quite deliberate.

Some of the faculty at Starr King tried to convert me to The Gospel of ARAOMC (herein after simply referred to as The Gospel), but once they saw I had questions they either couldn't or wouldn't answer, they left me alone – happy to take my money and give me a degree, but certainly not allow me into the inner circle of the Elect.

By nature, I am deeply suspicious of anything presented to me as gospel – something presented as inherently and obviously the truth, something that simply can't be questioned or exposed to critical inquiry. The way this mindset is revealed is simply to ask the question: "What are the biases, flaws, and weaknesses in your theory/beliefs/worldview?"

If you can tell me those, I'm more than willing to discuss what you are proposing. If not, then No thank you very much.

But any Gospel is not about truth, it is about belief. Anytime I asked questions about weaknesses or flaws in The Gospel, I was met with either puzzled looks, or the subject was changed.

I was written off as an old white guy who just didn't "get it". Maybe. But I get lots of things just fine, and blind belief just isn't in my repertoire, or in UU history and theology either.

Writing off people because of their social locations is just plain lazy. It's a form of ad hominem argument, as is claiming that your arguments are valid because of YOUR social location at some place on the power hierarchy.

In any case, Starr King was rife with cliques, the Oppression Olympics, students literally getting in another student's face because of their whiteness, or cisness, or some flawed identity. It could be ugly, and the administration finally had the sense to tamp it down, but only after much damage was done. I pretty much ignored it as I was there to learn to be a minister, something there was less teaching about than you might imagine for a divinity school.

And then the President of the school retired, and it came time to select a new one. And that got really ugly. Several observers – who I will not name for their protection – believe that professors were purged and students were denied their degrees because someone blew the whistle on the discriminatory and unethical actions of the outgoing President in overriding the decision of the Search Committee to select her replacement.

You can read about it in UU World – which is a somewhat impartial version of the events and their aftermath.

https://www.uuworld.org/articles/really-happened-starr-king

Read the comments, especially those of long time UU's in leadership.

Here's more:

https://www.danielharper.org/yauu/2015/01/kurt-kuhwalds-thoughts-on-starr-king/

https://www.uuworld.org/articles/two-sksm-professors-resign

As always, read and make up your own mind. Free religion, remember?

I think it's obvious that the school's President and Board reacted just like a corporation of the old white men they claim to be different from. The spin doctors came out in force. People's lives were seriously messed with, and without any due process. Faculty resigned and students left. Many who stayed kept their heads down, and minimized their connections with the school while struggling to acquire their degrees so they could get the credential and get out. There was no restitution. A lot of damage was done, and never made whole again. Academic, ministerial and institutional authority was abused in the service of power.

And to this day, those issues of the abuse of power have never been addressed. "Time to move on and let the healing begin" is the mantra. Shining the light of truth? Restorative justice? Don't make me laugh. It hurts too fucking much.

Functionally, this has meant that the public abuse of power has become normalized and... sanctified... in UU circles. Not that this is anything new. The UUMA, the UUA and MFC, have always been tainted with cronyism and various misuses and abuses of power.

Abusing Power as Theological Error

Let's go back to The Gospel for a moment. At its core, ARAOMC sees all power as hierarchical. Therefore, the solution to oppression is just a matter of flipping the hierarchy and placing those on the bottom on the top for a while, or forever. (This is also called centering, in the parlance of the believers.)

I assert that this is a structural problem inherent in ARAOMC. A problem made worse by the observation that the oppressed seem to have internalized their own experience of the abuses of power so deeply that they seem incapable of doing anything but repeating them. Which is tragic. And even worse, it doesn't break the cycle of abuse of power.

If you see all human relations as hierarchical power relationships to be overturned, then the way you will use power is defined by the view that power is not to be shared with those who don't agree with you. This is also not a very generous view of other human beings, who are way more complicated than ARAOMC dogma would have you believe. It also violates the basic ethical principle of reciprocity.

And as Thandeka pointed out years ago, it falls into the old Calvinist trap of condemning people by their very nature.

Another trap this kind of reductionist thinking creates is the binary trap. Racist/anti-racist, cis/queer, white/BIPOC, and other dualisms become self-reinforcing/codependent binaries in constant struggle – with no real way out of the hall of mirrors they create. Human beings have multiple, fluid, and complex identities that deserve respect and honoring, no matter who they are.

Power is always relational and situational, not permanently affixed to social location, nor some kind of cultural Matrix cast in stone. Any human being can misuse and abuse power – and doing so in the name of some moral or religious end is perhaps the most egregious of such abuses.

I contend that the abuse of power has always been part of the culture of leadership in the UUMA and UUA, and it no longer being abused by a bunch of "old white men", but by the group of religious radicals that has replaced them– and who are not liberal, but reactionary and illiberal.

And further, I contend that their current abuses deeply undermine the moral authority of our faith and our broader social justice efforts.

Because the claims being made against the dominant culture are ones of abuses of power, you cannot abuse power to "fight" or "dismantle" that culture and claim the moral high ground. Doing so negates any moral or spiritual superiority you may have, because you are guilty of the very thing you claim to be against.

It's called hypocrisy. And this is not just one of the simple hypocrisies we all engage in our daily lives, but a deep hypocrisy that hides behind a masquerade of justice.

It is a profound theological error as well.

Regulatory Capture and the MFC

Regulatory capture is a form of government failure which occurs when a regulatory agency, created to act in the public interest, instead advances the commercial or political concerns of special interest groups that dominate the industry or sector it is charged with regulating.

For years, the MFC has been a select committee of gatekeepers into UU ministry. Its processes were not transparent and not accountable. Their decisions were guided by a set of conscious and unconscious biases towards women, LGBTQIA+, class origins, and BIPOC. That changed because of social pressures towards equality, diversity, and inclusion. This has been a great and necessary thing.

But then a not-so-curious thing happened. Over the period of a few decades, the MFC became ideological gatekeepers, suppressing intellectual and theological diversity. To pass the MFC into fellowship, you must totally agree with ARAOMC dogma, and if you are white, hetero, and cis, you must confess and do repentance for your multiple pernicious identities.

Disagree with this shameful and flawed ideology in the slightest, and you can forget about a career in parish ministry, or being Fellowshipped.

The MFC controls the fellowshipping process in a way that is still not transparent, still not accountable, and is driven by ideological conformity. (They see it as theological purity, I'm sure.) Instead of changing a flawed process, believers in The Gospel have simply used it towards their own ends – to gain power and control of the narrative.

As a result, the UUMA, the UUA, and the MFC leadership are now totally dominated by those who agree with ARAOMC dogma, who have slowly stacked the deck and cast out, or driven out, any dissenters.

This is not the honest acquisition of power, but shady business. Same as it ever was.

And now, having stacked the deck, they claim the game is fair and that there is agreement and consensus in our faith. But imposed ideological conformity is neither.

Abuse of Power as Culture, Pt. II: Winning Ugly

There have been many abuses of power at the UUMA and the UUA. In the past, the UUMA has swept many abuses of ministerial power under the rug, failed to censure or dismiss ministers guilty of sexual misconduct, financial malfeasance, etc. Departing UUA Staff members have recently voted each other lovely severance packages. You don't have to dig very deep to find the abuse and misuse of power in our leadership.

And then there is the coup that took place in 2017 shortly after the hiring controversy and the resignation of the Rev. Peter

Morales. And yes, it was a coup. The reactionaries lost patience and took over the Board. In the ensuing years, believers in The Gospel have discarded any process that could challenge their power – parliamentary procedure and due process to name a couple. They have instituted on-the-fly moderation at GA, shutting down dissenting voices and controlling the outcome of voting. (Nothing new at GA, even pre-coup.) They change the rules to suit their ends, claiming that all past processes are tainted by White Supremacy Culture.

They abuse power to serve their vision. A noble vision in many ways. But abusing power is abusing power, no matter who does it.

It isn't different this time, and it isn't different because of who is abusing power. Meet the new boss, same as the old boss.

By Their Fruits Ye Shall Know Them

True spiritual and moral power is not about being in charge, taking the reins of power and telling people what to do and how to act. That flawed understanding is deeply embedded in ARAOMC dogma, and we now see the results.

The UUMA has censured one of its members for daring to ask questions, claiming harm without offering evidence, and dismissing several of our principles and sources as tools of WSC.

The UUA is beginning to "instruct" our congregations and fellowships that their primary focus is the rooting out of WSC from their hearts and minds and souls, in clear violation of congregational polity and again, against our principles and sources.

The hypocrisy and arrogance of this fundamentalist approach are stunning.

Social change cannot be dictated from the top, and each of us must be free to engage in the struggle for liberation in our own way, for our own reasons, and by our own choosing. That is what free religion is all about.

Fundamentalism and the Loss of Trust

Do I trust my fundamentalist coreligionists to provide honest testimony, as they see it, to their pain and suffering? Absolutely.

Do I trust my fundamentalist coreligionists to provide pastoral care and counseling to the broken and wounded among us? Absolutely.

Do I trust my fundamentalist coreligionists with power? Not a bit.

Do I trust them to lead our faith into the future in a way that honors our UU lineage and polity? NO.

And not just because of their extreme and uncompromising ideological positions on racism, oppression, and other issues.

My observation is that they have repeatedly demonstrated that they can't be trusted with the power vested in them by our congregations. They have used dishonest means to gain that power, and dishonest means to keep it. They seek to govern without the consent of the governed.

They are trying to turn a free religion into a fundamentalist religion, and that is a grave theological error that is in direct contradiction to both our Unitarian and Universalist heritages. This new fundamentalism is not Unitarian Universalism.

Universalism was a movement against the fundamentalist view that humanity was divided into the saved and the damned. Unitarianism opposed fundamentalisms of all kinds in the name of religious freedom. Both were against hierarchies of religious power that dictated belief and action, as is our humanist heritage.

What's Next?

I honestly don't know.

I don't disagree with the goals, only the theory and methods. And wielding religion and politics together has a disastrous history.

If we become a shrill and illiberal faith, I believe we are doomed to irrelevance. There are great challenges facing our world and humanity and all life on Earth, and many of us feel that the direction being taken by our leadership is making the finding of solutions more difficult, if not impossible.

Fighting religious fundamentalism is hard, and harder when they have power, control the narrative and the channels of communication, and misuse their authority. This is even more painful when they are your coreligionists, and they claim to represent you.

I think that the UUA and the UUMA will not be interested in answering these charges, nor are they interested in bringing this conversation "down" into our congregations for extended debate about this shift in our faith.

Orthodoxy by fiat is now the order of the day. Having taken power, they will not relinquish it without a fight. They are utterly convinced of their rightness, and of the error of all who question them.

Where we go next must be up to our congregations, decided in a wider discussion, not by a small group of reactionaries. I hope this can be accomplished, but I fear any such movement will be squashed.

But I think it behooves those of us who have faith in Unitarian Universalism to try.

Appendix 1.2: "I vs. We" by Jim Aikin

Classical liberalism is the belief that the individual is, or ought to be, autonomous. "Liberal" means "free." Liberals believe that, wherever possible, the individual ought to be free to make [his/her/their] own decisions and choose [his/her/their] own actions.

As an aside, normally I approve of the use of "they" and "their" to refer to single persons of unknown gender, but in that particular sentence, "their" runs the risk of implying something about membership in a group. Hence the awkward workaround.

Liberalism was pretty much invented in the 18th century. The power of the church was weakening, and as people moved to the cities they found themselves dealing with hordes of strangers. The customs that had worked in small villages no longer worked very well.

The idea of individual freedom could hardly have arisen in feudal society, because feudalism was based on a sense of mutual obligation among members of a small community. The same thing is true of tribal cultures worldwide. You know the people around you. You know their expectations, and they know yours. In a tribal culture, "go your own way" is a dangerous idea. It would rend the close-knit fabric of your world.

There is inevitably a tension between individual freedom and group solidarity. A society that goes to either extreme is cruel and dysfunctional. If individual freedom is elevated as the most exalted value, we have anarchy. I know there are people who consider themselves anarchists, but I'm pretty sure they don't get it. Anarchy means you can be run down by a speeding car, because there are no police. At the other extreme, where group solidarity is the highest value, you have totalitarianism. The people in authority tell you what to do, and you have no choice but to obey.

To a lover of freedom, people who embrace group solidarity are sheep, puppets, or zombies. To people who feel that group membership is vital, a lover of freedom is a serious threat, not just to individuals but to the survival and health of the entire group. The goal of the two factions (human happiness) is the same, but they define the conditions that will lead to happiness in very different ways.

The strife that has disrupted Unitarian-Universalism over the past decade is due precisely to a conflict between these two views. I happen to be firmly in the liberal camp, but I want to take a step back and look at the situation dispassionately and analytically. I'm aware that fans of group solidarity may feel that a painstaking logical analysis is a danger. I can't help that. Swing with me for a minute.

Unitarianism has been, for quite a long time, a liberal religion — if it's a religion at all, but we'll leave that debate for another time. The idea in Unitarianism has always been that you're free to believe what you like. The community has historically embraced free-thinkers.

During my lifetime (I'm in my 70s), liberals have pushed strongly for equal rights for marginalized groups — first African-Americans and other racial groups, then gay men and Lesbians, and more recently trans-identified people. This is an important and healthy development! But while considerable progress has been made, we're still a long way from a truly just and equal society.

Identity politics is, at root, the idea that when people who share some defining characteristic come together, they're stronger together, politically and socially, than they would be as individuals. The move toward organized labor (which I firmly support) was an early example of identity politics in action, as was the women's suffrage movement.

What has happened in recent years is that the people in marginalized groups have gotten frustrated that there hasn't been more progress. They have banded together in what we might call affinity groups in order to press for faster and more sweeping social changes.

The difficulty is this: People who have gathered together as a group can feel attacked by people who place a high value on individualism. A labor union, to take an easy example, only works when every worker is required to join the union. So-called right-to-work laws (which I vehemently oppose) undercut the ability of a union to accomplish what it hopes to accomplish.

Something similar seems to be happening in Unitarian-Universalism. Our national organization, the UUA, has been taken over by a group who are not committed in any way to individual liberty. They feel it's old-fashioned. In a nutshell, they view the traditional liberal slant of Unitarianism as a threat. They fervently believe in the value of group solidarity, because they have become frustrated at the slow pace of social change.

When you look at it through this lens, suddenly the strong reactions to Todd Eklof's book *The Gadfly Papers* make a lot more sense. Within a day of the book's release, a couple of hundred UU ministers signed an Open Letter denouncing the book. It's clear that most of them hadn't read the book before they attacked it.

To someone who places a high value on the thoughts and opinions of the individual, this behavior was shocking and incomprehensible. How could you possibly denounce a book you hadn't read? For that matter, how could you even recommend that others not read a book? No matter how wrong-headed a book may be, reading it is useful. (I own a copy of *Mein Kampf*, for instance.)

But to a person who values "we" above "I," attacking a book without having read it is perfectly sensible. If a member of your affinity group tells you a book is bad, your desire to remain with the group will assure you that going along with the group is the right thing to do. In fact, showing how vigorous you are in agreeing with the group's view (the pejorative term for this behavior is "virtue signaling") is important. You don't want to look like a backslider!

The book was attacked as being "ableist" and "transphobic," among other terms, even though there wasn't a word in it that could possibly be interpreted in those terms. But to a person who has embraced the "we" point of view, what's important is to identify with and embrace one's affinity group, which in a broad sense would include both trans people and people with disabilities. An attack on any member of the group is perceived as an attack on the group as a whole.

Eklof took aim squarely at Robin DiAngelo's book *White Fragility*. DiAngelo is a guiding light of this particular "we" group. So an attack on DiAngelo was interpreted as an attack on the group, and thus on the hopes and aspirations of everybody in the group, including trans and disabled people.

The Open Letter repeatedly claimed that *The Gadfly Papers* caused "harm" — yet the nature of the alleged harm was never explained. To anyone who values the right of the individual to make up [his/her/their] own mind, this was a grotesque cognitive failure. But to "we" people, questioning DiAngelo's views was, in and of itself, causing "harm." No explanation was necessary; the "harm" was writ on every page.

The result of this controversy is that Unitarian-Universalism is in big trouble. Membership is declining. Congregations are riven by strife.

Ironically, Eklof's book proposes what could be a very viable way out of the mess. Unitarianism and Universalism ought to go their separate ways. Let the Unitarians remain in the "I" camp, celebrating individual differences, and let the "we" crowd have Universalism to do with as they will.

I'm a cynic, so I anticipate that the "we" crowd won't like this idea. One of the features of a group solidarity culture is that groups tend to think that everybody ought to do it their way. This trend is easily seen in certain branches of Christianity and Islam. If you feel that your way is the only right way, letting other people choose their own values is tantamount to an admission of defeat. If they're not doing it your way, that's an implicit attack on your values. Well, we can't have that, can we?

I'm still a liberal, but I'm also a socialist. I understand the need for people to come together and work together for the common good. In my view, each situation, each conflict as it arises, has to be considered separately. A one-size-fits-all solution doesn't appeal to me. The difficulty I see is that those who embrace a "we" solution to social problems may feel threatened by the idea that individual cases ought to be analyzed individually. A blanket "solution" is likely to be more appealing, even when the collateral damage is severe.

I don't see an easy path around this conflict. But I do think splitting Unitarianism off from Universalism would have some solid advantages.

Made in the USA
Las Vegas, NV
12 October 2022

57140604R00105